GO ▷ surf

Tim Baker

London, New York, Munich, Melbourne, Delhi

Project Editor **Richard Gilbert**
Editors **Tarda Davison-Aitkins, Alex Dick-Read**
Senior Art Editor **Susan St Louis**
Project Art Editor **Katie Eke**
Design by **On Fire**
Production Editors **Vania Cunha, Sarah Sherlock**
Production Controller **Inderjit Bhullar**
Managing Editor **Stephanie Farrow**
Managing Art Editor **Lee Griffiths**
Photography **Matt Oldfield**

DVD produced for Dorling Kindersley by
Scubazoo www.scubazoo.com
Director **Roger Munns**
Camera **Roger Munns, Russell Campbell**
Graphics **Jonni Isaacs**
Online editor **KB.Lai**
Voiceover **Michael Andersen**
Voiceover Recording **Nick Miller**
Music **Brollyman**

First published in Great Britain in 2007 by
Dorling Kindersley Limited
80 Strand
London WC2R 0RL

A Penguin Company

2 4 6 8 10 9 7 5 3 1

A CIP catalogue record for this book is available from
the British Library.

ISBN: 978-1-40531-822-8

Colour reproduction by Wyndeham Pre-Press, UK
Printed and bound in China by Hung Hing

Discover more at

www.dk.com

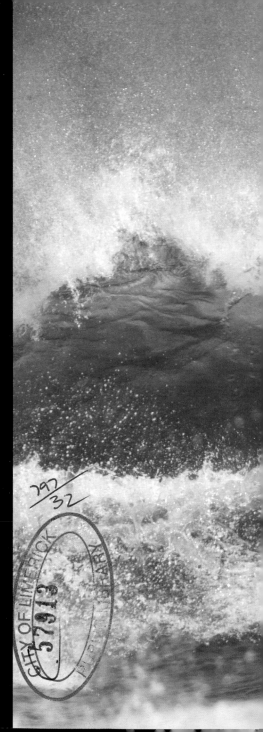

contents

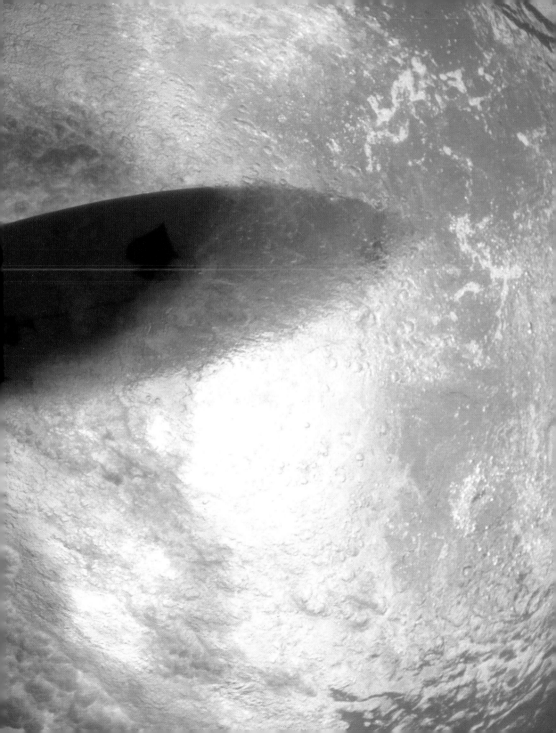

how to use this book and DVD

This fully integrated book and accompanying DVD are designed to inspire you to get in the water and start surfing. Watch the essential techniques on the DVD in crystal-clear, real-time footage, with key elements broken down in state-of-the-art digital graphics, and then read all about them, and more, in the book.

Using the book
Heading into the surf for the first time can seem a daunting prospect, so this book explains everything you need to know to go surfing with safety and confidence. Cross-references to the DVD are included on pages that are backed up by footage.

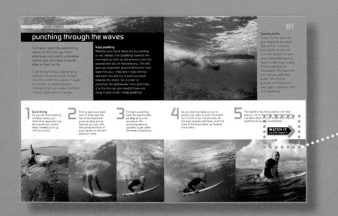

WATCH IT
see DVD chapter 3

Switch on the DVD
When you see this logo in the book, check out the action in the relevant chapter of the DVD.

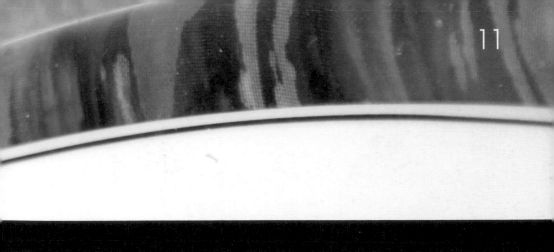

Using the DVD

Supporting the book with movie sequences and computer graphics, the DVD is the perfect way to see key techniques demonstrated in precise detail. Navigate to each subject using the main menu, and view sequences as often as you like to see how it's done!

Flick to the book

When you see this logo on the DVD, flick to the relevant page of the book to read all about it.

why surf ?

There is nothing like surfing. Breaking waves have always drawn mesmerized observers, and the art of riding them is a physical expression of that fascination. It involves bravery, endurance, and athleticism, but somehow it transcends the boundaries of sport in its expression of grace, beauty, and some intangible sense of rhythmic perfection.

Once you start surfing and you find yourself sitting out at sea, turning and stroking for a wave, you are placing yourself in the path of an irresistible force and the rest of your surfing life will be spent learning how to harness that energy most successfully. Sometimes dangerous, often violent as the water throws you around without mercy, you will find that it is at other times peaceful, almost spiritual, and always sensational.

After the very first time you take to the waves – tired, frustrated, sore in muscles you didn't know existed – you'll already be looking forward to your next session, most likely staring out to sea with a grin, water dripping from your nose, and feeling wonderfully alive. This is your first dose of "surf stoke" and in all likelihood, it will never leave you.

Happy surfing!

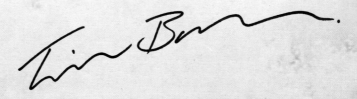

go for it!

coming up...

The goal: 18–21

So you want to surf? Hurtling shorewards on a peeling wave, with foam at your heels and spray in your face, is a unique thrill, but it doesn't happen over night. Sample some visual and literary inspiration to get you in the mood.

World of surfing: 22–31

From ancient Polynesian royalty to highly paid 21st-century professionals, surfers have come a long way in 1000 years or so. And you are about to re-trace that epic voyage of discovery.

The surfing environment: 32–39

Tides, winds, swells, weather maps, reefs, rips, and channels – there's a whole world of ocean theory that will help you on your surfing journey. Know before you go and you'll save yourself a lot of struggle.

catching a wave

Walking down the beach as the first rays of sunlight peak over the horizon, the sand feels cold and crunchy under your feet. The air tastes fresh despite a thin, salty mist, and the beach is deserted but for you and your friends.

The waves are clean and peaky, brushed by a gentle off-shore breeze, and refracting a thousand shades of orange and gold from the rising sun. Your heart-rate accelerates with anticipation as you trot across the sand, and the kiss of the ocean sends a shiver through your body as you wade out, pushing your board beside you through the rushing whitewater. Then you're lying down, breathing hard, feeling your muscles stretch as you paddle, blood starting to pump. The sharp chill of your first duck dive finally awakens all your senses – immediately your mind is clear, sparkling with a fresh awareness.

Pushing through rows of whitewater you find the channel where an outgoing current carries you further out. Suddenly you're in the line-up, behind the breaking waves, a peaceful place where the undulating swells stand tall before toppling on the reef. Further in is chaos, out here is calm, and a fine line between the two is the path you seek to tread.

continued ❯

catching a wave (continued)

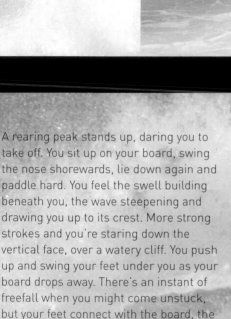

A rearing peak stands up, daring you to take off. You sit up on your board, swing the nose shorewards, lie down again and paddle hard. You feel the swell building beneath you, the wave steepening and drawing you up to its crest. More strong strokes and you're staring down the vertical face, over a watery cliff. You push up and swing your feet under you as your board drops away. There's an instant of freefall when you might come unstuck, but your feet connect with the board, the rail and fins grab the wave, and suddenly you're skimming fast down the face, feet planted firmly, sensing every bump on the surface.

A slight pressure on the balls of your feet sends you arcing off the bottom and swinging back up the wave as the lip starts to throw and curl above. You stall, leaning hard on your back foot, ducking and crouching down low. Suddenly you're in the tube, wrapped entirely by the clear curtain of a throwing lip.

Shifting your weight forwards brings you into perfect trim with the racing curl, speeding through the watery tunnel, staring at a spinning, almond-shaped eye of light up ahead. The tube begins to shrink and accelerate and you crouch lower, shifting your weight further forwards as the eye of light grows again and – BOOM! – you're back in daylight in a shower of spray, blinking and adrenalized. Harnessing the speed, you lean back on your heels into a smooth, arcing cutback, rebounding off the foam before kicking out onto the shoulder of the wave.

Your friends hoot their approval, your body tingles with adrenaline, and all you can think about is doing it again.

a brief history of surfing

Most surf historians agree that wave-riding was first practised by the ancient Polynesians, particularly the Tahitians and Hawaiians, and spread as they migrated across the Pacific over a thousand years ago. Surfing reached its cultural zenith in Hawaii, where it became ingrained in both ritual and legend.

Although Hawaiian culture was suppressed by European settlers in the 19th century, wave-riding was kept alive in the early stages of the 20th century by a handful of Waikiki beach boys. Fortunately for the world, one of them was an Olympic gold-medallist swimmer named Duke Kahanamoku, who gave surfing demonstrations as he toured the world. The Duke is revered as the father of modern surfing.

Today, Duke's legacy includes a World Tour for elite professional surfers, and a booming industry in fashion, music, and movies. Boards have evolved from enormous, solid wooden slabs, 3 m (10 ft) long and weighing 45 kg (100 lb) or more, to featherlight, high-performance surfcraft. Tow-in surfing, using high-powered jet-skis, is opening up massive open-ocean waves – the race is on for the first surfer to ride a 100-foot wave.

SURFING TIMELINE

1700s: surfing practised by Hawaiians of all ages and sexes, from royalty to commoners. Shorter "alaia" boards are used by most adults, and larger "olo" by royalty.

1820s: surfing virtually wiped **out** by European diseases and the spread of Christianity.

Early 1900s: Waikiki beach boys revive surfing in Hawaii. Writings of Jack London give exposure to the resurging sport.

1950s: Foam fibreglass boards are invented, resulting in boards that are lighter and more user-friendly.

1700

1800

1900

1950

c. 1000: stand-up surfing emerges in the Hawaiian islands.

1779: Europeans first encounter surfing as Captain Cook reaches Hawaii and Tahiti.

1910–20: Duke Kahanamoku's demonstrations are watched by thousands as he tours the USA, Australia, and New Zealand.

1959: Hollywood film "Gidget" popularizes surfing, leading to an explosion in surfing itself, surf fashion, and music.

1960s: Longboarding is in its heyday.

Late-1960s: Boards are cut down to create shorter, more manoeuvreable surfcraft.

1980s: Innovative surfboard designs proliferate, with two and three fins added for thrust and stability.

2000: tow-in surfing emerges at the cutting edge of surfing.

1960   1970   1980   1990   2000   **NOW**

1966: "Endless Summer" film enchants the world with a tale of the surf traveller's restless search for the next wave.

1976: Professional surfing begins with the founding of the International Professional Surfers, which organizes the first world circuit.

1990s: Longboarding is revived as older surfers rediscover the grace of surfing on longer boards.

Estimates put the number of surfers at more than 20 million worldwide.

styles of surfing

The two main forms of surfboard riding are longboarding and shortboarding. Small, long, peeling waves are perfect for longboards, while larger, hollow, peaky reef or beachbreaks generally suit a shortboard better.

The longboard, typically 3 m (10 ft) in length, evolved from traditional Hawaiian surfboards, gradually incorporating more refined curves and lighter materials over time. Shortboards are typically 2 m (6½ ft) or less in length.

Shortboard revolution

The so-called "shortboard revolution" began in around 1966, when adventurous surfers began to literally saw off and re-shape the front of their boards, in order to make them more manoeuvrable.

In a few years, surfboards shrank from 3 m (10 ft) down to 2 m (6½ ft) or less, and each generation since has developed more radical styles of surfing based around abrupt, high-speed direction changes, radical manoeuvres, and deep tube rides. In order to keep pace, boards have sprouted two, then three or more fins, and have become ever thinner, lighter, and more curved.

WATCH IT
see DVD chapter 1

Longboard revival
A longboard resurgence occurred in the late 1990s as many older surfers returned to the waves and rediscovered the joys of the simple, uncluttered glide, grace, and flow of longboarding. Since then, many of the experimental designs from the 1970s and 1980s have been rediscovered, such as the "fish" and twin-fin designs.

Today, surfers ride all manner of surfcraft, alternating from short to long and back again as the conditions require. The choice is yours, but as a wise surfer once said – there is no such thing as a bad surf, just the wrong choice of equipment.

surfing offshoots

Many variations and offshoots of surfing have developed over time. Some, like bodysurfing, have been around for as long as there have been waves, and others, such as kitesurfing and bodyboarding, have been developed as surf technology has pushed the boundaries of the sport. If riding a surfboard isn't for you, or if you fancy broadening your surfing horizons, there is no shortage of other ways to experience the magic of surfing.

a

b

a Bodysurfing
Undoubtedly the first way to ride waves was bodysurfing, and it is the most accessible offshoot if you can swim. At its extreme, elite bodysurfers ride huge, dangerous waves like Hawaii's legendary Pipeline with nothing but swimming trunks and flippers.

b Bodyboarding
Soft foam bodyboards are popular as a stepping stone towards surfing. They are a fun way for beginners to get used to wave-riding, while experts use them to catch outrageous tube rides, and perform a dazzling array of aerial manoeuvres, flips, and spins.

c Kitesurfing
Developed as an offshoot of windsurfing, kitesurfing is a dynamic form of wave-riding. Boards are short and the rider holds handles attached to cables and a kite. Typically ridden on flat water or waves with speed and agility, they can be used to catch incredible air time.

d Windsurfing
An offshoot of surfing and sailing, windsurfing became popular in the 1980s, but has since faded with the onset of kitesurfing. Nonetheless, it remains an exciting way to harness the wind and waves.

c
d

Other forms of surfing

There are a number of lesser known, but still popular, variants of surfing:

- Kneeboarding – an almost-dying art that involves riding boards made especially for kneeling down. Short, wide, and flat, these boards are well-suited to deep tube-riding but have fallen in popularity, perhaps due to the rise of the foam bodyboard.

- Wave-skiing – the wave-ski resembles a small kayak that you sit on top of (rather than inside as you do when surf-kayaking), and propel using a paddle. The best wave-ski riders can surf waves as acrobatically as any board-rider.

- Stand-up paddleboarding – this ancient Hawaiian art has recently been revived. Riding an enormous board that is 3.5 m (12 ft) long, and armed with an oar, the surfer stands upright, and paddles the board like a canoe. Swells can be caught well before they break, with the oar being used to help steer by dragging and dipping it in the water.

- Tow-in surfing – high-powered jet-skis are used to tow big-wave riders into massive open-ocean waves, or "bomboras". Waves up to 18 m (60 ft) high are now regularly being ridden.

fit to surf

Surfing certainly helps your fitness, but getting into shape before you start will mean you have more fun when you hit the waves.

Be warned: you will use muscles that you may not ordinarily exercise. Your arms, shoulders, and back are used for paddling, and your abdominals and legs for standing up and manoeuvring your board. Strengthen these muscles to minimize early aches and pains.

Swimming proficiency

The primary skill essential for surfing, swimming is also the best way to improve your surf-specific fitness. Visit your local swimming pool and take some lessons. Learn proper technique and breathing, and practise relentlessly – build up the distance you can swim over several weeks. When you feel that you are ready, go for a few ocean swims in whatever you are likely to wear surfing – wetsuit and all, if necessary.

WATCH IT
see DVD chapter 1

Improving your fitness

Any form of exercise that increases aerobic fitness will help you in the surf, but there are also a number of activities that target specific areas:

- Skipping and beach-running are excellent for building lung capacity.

- Tai Chi, yoga, and boxing are good for improving upper body strength, reflexes, and flexibility.

- Balance boards and exercise balls can be used to improve balance.

- Meditation and visualization improve spacial awareness.

Skateboarding

A great way to learn the dynamics of surfing is to take up skateboarding. Practise on smooth, gentle slopes away from hazards.

- Learn to store speed in your body, go with the momentum of the board, and be aware of your lower body staying solid while your upper body remains loose.

learning to surf

It's important to learn some basic surf safety, techniques, and etiquette before you charge head-long into the breakers. A qualified surf instructor can teach you all this and more. A series of six or more lessons at the start of your surfing "career" will greatly accelerate your progress.

Choosing a surf school

You can join a group class of ten or so students or, for a greater outlay, have a private, one-on-one class. If it's within your budget, a few group classes to start with, followed by a few one-on-one sessions, is ideal.

A significant part of your first surf lesson will be spent on the beach, learning surfing theory and becoming familiar with your board. Don't be over-eager to charge into the waves. This knowledge will prove invaluable when you come to navigate your way through a churning ocean.

If you don't live near a surf beach, travelling to a surf destination with its own surf school for a couple of weeks can be a great way to start your surfing journey.

Checking accreditation

Surf schools have been a boom industry in recent years and there are many operators of varying quality. The International Surfing Association (ISA) has a globally recognised accreditation course for surf coaches, and most countries have similar surf coaching qualifications. Be sure your surf coach and school are properly accredited and have the relevant local permits to operate.

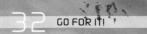
how waves are formed

Waves are pure energy. They pass through water but do not transport the water itself, only moving through it like a pulse sent through a length of rope. These pulses of energy form ocean swells and are born in storm systems out in the open ocean, often travelling huge distances before ending their journey by breaking over a distant beach or reef.

Lifecycle of a swell

A swell is a series of large, evenly spaced waves generated by weather systems at sea. Over long expanses of ocean, the larger swells overtake and absorb smaller swells in their path. This process results in swells becoming more organized, well-spaced, and well-defined. When swells approach a coast or reef, the bottom of the swell brushes the ocean floor, causing the swell to rise higher until the crest spills down the face of the wave. Then we have surf.

Storm

Wind

Wave formation
Storms generate winds that blow over the ocean to generate swell. The longer and harder they blow, the bigger the swell.

Origin
The storm acts like a pebble dropped in a pond, sending out ripples of energy in concentric circles.

Chaotic energy
At first the ripples are small, random windswells packed closely together.

Wave regularity
As the swells travel through the ocean, they order themselves into larger, even swell lines.

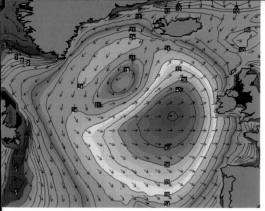

Significant wave height (ft)

0 1 2.5 5 7.5 10 15 20 30 40 50

Using WAM charts

The colours on the chart indicate the size of swell in the ocean. These measurements are gathered by satellites, wave buoys that sit in the ocean and collect data, and reports from ships at sea. All of this data gives us a fairly accurate indication of the swell conditions at sea, which in turn tells us how big the waves are likely to be on our coastlines.

Reading weather maps

The lines on a weather map, known as isobars, represent areas of equal atmospheric pressure, and reveal the direction and strength of winds. In the northern hemisphere, winds circulate anti-clockwise around a low-pressure system (L), and clockwise around a high-pressure system (H). The reverse is true for the southern hemisphere. The closer together the isobars, the stronger the wind.

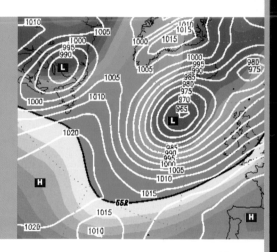

WATCH IT
see DVD chapter 1

Waves heighten
As the swells begin to brush the ocean floor, they slow down and push upwards.

Waves break
As the bottom of the swell slows down, the peak overtakes it and begins to break.

Energy dissipates
Waves reach the shore, re-shaping the coastline. Outward-rushing water creates rips and currents.

how waves react

The type of wave created when ocean swells reach the coastline depends on several factors. The off-shore depth and shape of the ocean floor, the geography of the coast it collides with, the wind conditions, and the tides are all crucial.

The features of a coastline can be split into three categories – beach break, reef break, and point break – and each have their own unique characteristics.

How the wind affects waves

Wind strength and direction is critical to the quality of waves. Usually, surfers look for light, off-shore winds – blowing from land out to sea – since this creates clean, peeling waves. On-shore winds cause messy, choppy conditions that are more difficult to surf. Side-shore winds blow parallel to the coast and can create tricky ridges, known as wind-chop, in the waves, which are difficult to negotiate.

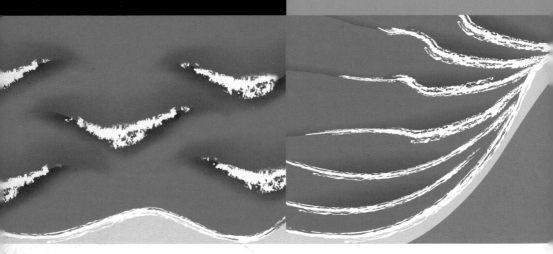

Anatomy of a beach break
When advancing swells meet sandy beaches, the waves peak and break quite randomly thanks to shifting sandbanks. This can make them tricky to judge, but they offer plenty of opportunities for learner surfers to catch waves away from crowds.

Anatomy of a point break
Point breaks peel along the edge of headlands, fingers of land, or any protruding geographical feature. They are characterized by long, evenly peeling waves that wrap around the protrusion, like spokes around the hub of a wheel.

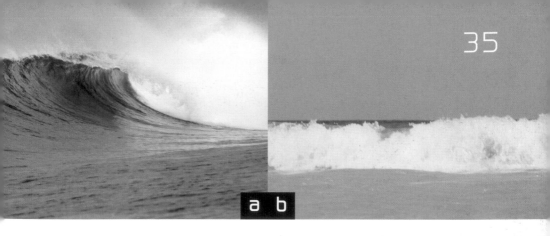

a b

Peeling wave
Surfers look for evenly peeling waves, where the wave breaks cleanly in one direction. The surfer can ride the clean face of the wave just ahead of the breaking whitewater, which is also known as the curl.

Close-out wave
Waves that break together in a straight line are known as crumbling or close-out waves. They are useful for beginners learning how to paddle, and catch waves, but are no good once you're able to ride the clean face of the wave.

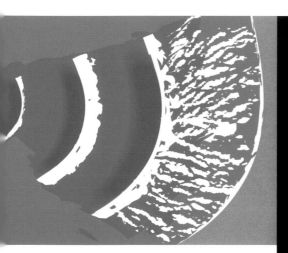

Anatomy of a reef break
Reef breaks break over coral, lava, or rocky reefs, and usually produce abrupt, hollow waves. Such conditions leave little margin for error, so are best suited to experienced surfers.

How the tide affects waves
Tides raise and lower the depth of the ocean at the coastline, which can dramatically alter the character of a break. A peeling, hollow point break at low tide might be transformed into a soft, crumbling wave at high tide. Tides can also influence the strength and intensity of a swell. Waves may break with more force on an incoming tide, and become smaller and inconsistent on an outgoing tide.

Tides run on a roughly 12-hour cycle, influenced by the moon, so there is a difference of around 6 hours between high and low tide. Monitor the conditions as the tides change and learn to recognize the types of waves that suit your level of ability.

anatomy of the line-up

The more you know and understand about the dynamics of the line-up, the better you'll be able to navigate your way around it. Currents and rips can be dangerous but can also work in your favour, enabling you to spend less time paddling and more time riding waves.

Choosing a break

The dynamics of the surf vary according to the type of break you're on – beach break, reef break, or point break. For your first forays into the surf, look for a gentle beach break close to shore with a sandy bottom, where the whitewater rolls down the wave face, rather than dumping abruptly.

Avoid rocks, reefs, strong rips and currents, and more challenging waves suited to more experienced surfers. Assess the conditions and decide whether you are really ready to charge out there. A good rule of thumb is, if you wouldn't swim out, maybe you shouldn't paddle out.

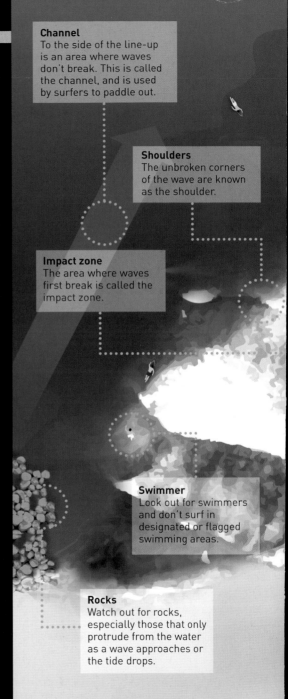

Channel
To the side of the line-up is an area where waves don't break. This is called the channel, and is used by surfers to paddle out.

Shoulders
The unbroken corners of the wave are known as the shoulder.

Impact zone
The area where waves first break is called the impact zone.

Swimmer
Look out for swimmers and don't surf in designated or flagged swimming areas.

Rocks
Watch out for rocks, especially those that only protrude from the water as a wave approaches or the tide drops.

Peak
The point at which the wave begins to crest, just before it breaks, is known as the peak.

Surfer on the wave
The surfer on the wave has right of wave, so always paddle wide of the line-up on your way back out.

Surfer paddling out
When riding waves, be alert for other surfers paddling out, and keep your board under control when you catch a wave.

Rip current
Water rushes back out to sea through channels at the edge of the break, forming rip currents that can sometimes by dangerous. If you get caught in a strong rip, always paddle across the rip, back into the break.

Direction of the wave
Waves peel in one direction – either to the left or the right – according to the topography of the sea floor. From the perspective of a surfer in the line-up facing the shore, a wave that peels from left to right is called a right-hander, and a wave peeling from right to left is known as a left-hander.

Sea-floor topography
The depth and steepness of the ocean floor will influence how waves break.

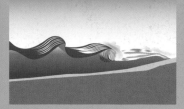

Sloping ocean floor
When waves move over a gently sloping ocean floor into shallower water, they slow down and lose power. This produces more gentle surf, perfect for learners.

Stepped ocean floor
When waves travel from deep to shallow water very suddenly, they break with enormous force. These waves are best left to the experts.

surfing etiquette

It's important to learn some basic surfing etiquette early on. Surfing is governed by an unwritten code that has been passed down through the generations.

As a learner, it is up to you to stay out of the way of more experienced surfers. Surfing in quieter waters, away from the main pack of surfers, is usually a good idea when starting out. Make sure you give respect and plenty of latitude to more experienced and local surfers at the break you are surfing.

Paddling out

It's important to paddle out to the line-up without endangering yourself or fellow surfers. Consider the following:

- The surfer on the wave has right of way over surfers paddling out. If you find yourself caught inside by a breaking wave with a surfer hurtling towards you, always paddle towards the whitewater, away from the clean face of the wave where the surfer is heading. Don't try to paddle across the path of the surfer. This may mean you have to deal with buffeting from the whitewater, but it is better than being struck by a speeding surfboard.

- When you paddle out and are confronted by a breaking wave, don't throw your board away, since it could endanger other surfers. Instead learn to duck dive or turn turtle (see pages 80–81), and hold on to your board at all costs.

- Once you've finished riding a wave, always return to the line-up by paddling around the break, not through it, to avoid other surfers.

✓ Right of wave

The surfer who catches the wave first, or who is closest to the curl or the breaking part of the wave, has right of wave. You may occasionally see more experienced surfers breaking this rule, but that doesn't mean that you can too.

✗ Don't drop in

Never catch a wave that another surfer is already on. This is crucial when you are in the line-up with more experienced surfers, who may be hurtling along the unbroken wave face. The surfer on the left of the photograph is dropping in.

go get your gear

coming up...

Surfboards: 44–49

From longboards to shortboards, fish, mini-mals, and fun boards, there is a greater variety of wave-riding equipment available today than ever before. Find the board that suits your experience, ability, and physique.

Essential equipment: 50–55

There's a lot that goes into keeping you in the water and riding waves. Discover the wonderful world of surfing accessories and how to get the most from them.

Looking after it all: 56–59

Setting yourself up as a surfer can be a serious investment, so it makes sense to take steps to protect that investment. Learn how to care for your board and accessories to get years of use and enjoyment from them.

anatomy of the surfboard

Surfboard terminology can sometimes seem like a foreign language but understanding a few basic terms and concepts will help put you in the know. A good way to familiarize yourself with board anatomy is to study the planshape of a board – the outline of your surfboard when viewed from above.

Tail
The rear of the board is known as the tail.

Rail
The edges on both sides of the board are known as rails.

Legrope plug
This is the point to which you attach your legrope string.

Longboard design
Usually around 3 m (10 ft) long, and straight for paddling speed and stability, longboards have a gentle rocker (the bottom curve from nose to tail).

Planshape

Profile

Rocker

Single-fin
V-bottom

Fin technology

Different fins make a board suitable for different conditions. Bigger fins provide more drive but make the board stiffer and harder to turn. If the fins have hard edges, the board will turn stiffer and faster, while softer edges make it turn looser. Screw fins are good for travelling and allow you to try different fin types.

Tail technology

Different tail shapes have different performance characteristics. Square and swallow tails suit sharp, abrupt turns, while round tails suit smoother surfing, and pin tails are generally used on longer, big-wave boards for speed and wider turns.

Square tail

Swallow tail

Round tail

Pin tail

Nose
The nose is the front of the board.

Deck
The top of your board is known as the deck.

Shortboard design

Approximately 2 m (6½ ft) long, with a curved planshape, shortboards are designed for tight, fast direction changes and the full range of modern manoeuvres.

Planshape

Profile

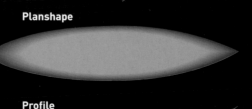

Double concave tri-fin bottom

types of surfboard

WATCH IT
see DVD chapter 1

The surfboard market has never been as wide and varied as it is today. A revival in so-called retro models means surfers have a greater choice of boards than ever before – short or long, fish or egg (a design from the 1960s with a rounded nose and tail), single- or twin-fin, or thruster.

Most surfers who learn at a surf school will start on a soft beginner board, and something like this could well suit you for the first year or more of your surfing life. Eventually, though, you might aspire to a board with greater performance attributes. The foam and fibreglass boards that most surfers ride are stiffer and more rigid, thus faster and more responsive than beginner boards.

Fish design
Constructed from timber veneer, this is a modern make-over of a popular 1970s design, now back in fashion for its speed, paddling power, and in small-wave performance.

Single-fin board
1970s single-fin designs have recently regained popularity. They paddle well, are fast down the line, and good in the tube.

Thruster board
Fast, light and manoeuvrable, the modern, three-finned thruster board is favoured by most intermediate to advanced surfers.

Mini-mal design
This is a short version of the longboard, or "malibu", hence the name mini-mal. It is stable for beginners, and not too heavy or hard to handle.

Longboard
The longboard is stable and easy to ride, but can be heavy and unwieldy to get out through the surf.

Beginner board
Soft foam boards designed for beginners are safe, stable, and great fun to learn on.

choosing the right board

When you come to select a surfboard, your main choices are the dimensions – length, width, and thickness – and its shape. Longboards are stable and buoyant, and easy to stand up on, but are heavier and more unwieldly than shortboards to get through the surf. Shortboards are lighter, thinner, and less stable, but better for high-performance surfing, and easier to duck dive.

For most beginners, a mini-mal or similar will provide a good compromise between stability and manoeuvrability, since it is thick, wide, and stable, but not too heavy or unwieldy. A board that is 2–2.5 m (6½– 8 ft) long, around 50 cm (20 in) wide, and around 7 cm (3 in) thick, will suit most adult learners. Talk to an experienced surfer or surfboard shaper for more precise specifications. A second-hand board in good condition should be more than adequate in the early stages of your surfing life.

As you grow more confident and competent, your board tastes will become more specific and eventually you may want to order a custom board from a shaper, or experiment with a variety of equipment to see what best suits you. Where possible, try to test-ride a board before you buy.

The surfing time-machine

A handy way to choose the right board is to "place" your ability on the evolutionary path of surfing.

• If you are standing up in the whitewater and riding straight in to the beach, you are at the same level as the first surfers, who rode long, stable boards. The modern equivalent is a soft beginner board.

• If you are starting to angle across the unbroken wave face, as surfers started doing in the early 1900s, try a modern longboard or mini-mal.

• If you are starting to perform your first competent turns, try a shorter board, as surfers began to use in the late 1960s.

• If you are graduating to sharper turns, try a fish or other 1970s twin-fin design.

• If you like going fast, getting tubed, and drawing long, smooth lines, try a sleek 1970s pin-tail single-fin board.

• If you can link manoeuvres together smoothly, try a modern three-finned thruster, the design that swept the surfing world in the 1980s.

types of wetsuit

Wetsuit technology has come a long way in the past ten years, and even extreme, cold-weather suits up to 5-mm thick afford full freedom of movement. Choose the right suit for local conditions and make sure the fit is snug without being too tight.

Wetsuit tips

- Dark colours will absorb the sun's heat and keep you warmer, which is why most wetsuits are black. In cold water, taped seams will reduce the amount of water-flow through your suit and help keep you warmer too. In extreme cold, rubber hoods, gloves, and booties may be needed.

- A full-length wetsuit with long arms and legs is known as a "steamer" and comes in 3–5 mm thicknesses. Long or short sleeves for various water temperatures and climates are also available.

- For warmer climates, "spring suits" come in short- and long-arm varieties, with short legs. Tube suits, or "short johns", have no arms and short legs, to ward off wind-chill and provide protection from shallow reefs.

- A lycra rash vest can be worn under your wetsuit to eliminate chafing. The wetsuit should be rinsed in freshwater and hung to dry after each use, out of direct sunlight.

surf kit for warm weather

There is nothing like the pleasure of surfing in only boardshorts or a bikini. In warm water, the freedom of movement in a simple swimsuit makes for easier, more enjoyable surfing. A lycra rash vest can be worn to avoid rash from your surfboard and sunburn.

Surfing in hot climates can also take its toll. Try to surf in the early morning and late afternoon to avoid the worst of the midday sun. Remember to re-hydrate and be aware of the symptoms of sunstroke (dizziness and extreme fatigue).

What to look for

There are plenty of specialist products for warm-weather surfing that will help keep you in the water and stop you from getting sunburnt.

- Specialist surfing boardshorts and bikinis are made to withstand the demands of surfing – they are strong, durable, quick-drying, and not likely to fall off during your first wipeout.

- A white rash vest will reflect the sun's rays and stop you from burning. It will also protect you from sunstroke and rash from your board (caused by wax aggravating your skin when lying down on the board and paddling).

- Sunscreen should be liberally applied to exposed areas of skin before each surf. Look for types that are water-resistant for at least two hours, and at least factor SPF15.

- A hat and sunglasses are essential when spending long hours in the sun between surfs.

Walk into a surf shop and you may be overwhelmed by the array of products. Some are essential, others aren't. Here are a few tips to help you work out what gear you need, and how to care for it.

A surfboard represents quite an investment, so you should look after it carefully. Keep it in a cover, and always store it safely. Make sure you repair all dings (dents in your board) promptly to stop your board from absorbing water.

surfing extras

Care and repair
Surfboards with pointed noses should be fitted with a soft rubber noseguard to reduce the risk of injury. These are easy to apply using a special glue that comes with the noseguard. If you plan to travel with your board, it's a good idea to take a small ding repair kit. It will save you a lot of time and hassle, and prolong the life of your board. Check with your airline before you travel though, as some refuse to let passengers carry them as luggage because of their flammable nature.

Useful accessories

You don't need to arm yourself with every accessory under the sun, but a few essentials can make your life safer and easier, and prolong the life of your equipment.

- Safety-conscious surfers may choose to wear a surf-specific helmet in the sea.

- Straps or tie-downs are an easy and convenient way to tie your board to the roof of a car – whether it has a roofrack or not.

- A cover is essential when transporting your board. A soft, towelling stretch-cover will protect your board from minor dings on car journeys. Use a padded cover when flying. Coffin-style covers are great for multiple boards.

- When travelling by car, store wet gear in a large plastic box. This prevents saltwater from seeping into your car and causing rust. Use a smaller plastic container for fin keys, wax, wax combs, spare legrope strings, and sunscreen.

waxing your board

Wax is essential to stop you slipping on the deck of your board, and is available in both cold- and warm-water formulas. Cold-water wax is more easily applied in cold climates, but avoid applying both on the same board as they will slip against each other, making the board slippery. If you are travelling to different climates, carefully remove the old wax with hot water and a scraper, and apply a fresh coat.

Choosing where to wax

You need to wax every point that your feet are likely to touch while surfing, so wax right to the tail of the board, out to the rails, and up to where your chest rests when you're lying down.

Deck grip

You may decide to use deck grip, which is optional according to your personal preference. It is convenient if you don't happen to have wax with you, but can cause a rash, and most experienced surfers tend to prefer wax for traction, or just a back-foot tail pad.

Applying new wax

Apply wax in a brisk back and forth motion, creating an even cover of small lumps of wax. Avoid applying wax in a circular motion, since doing so can create larger lumps, and provides less traction.

Roughening old wax

Old coats of wax can be roughened up with the use of a wax comb, stick, or pointed stone. Drag the implement across the surface of the wax one way, and then at right angles to the original direction. If you find yourself stuck with an old coat of wax and no more wax or a comb, you can also roughen up the surface by rubbing sand into it.

legropes

A legrope is fixed to your board at one end and your ankle at the other, so that you stay close to it if you wipe out. They come in small- and big-wave models, in lengths of 2–4 m (6½–13 ft). A small-wave model will suffice for beginners.

1 Attaching your legrope
To attach your legrope to the board, you first need to create a loop of string through which to pass the railsaver. The simplest way to do this is with an overhand knot. Begin by doubling up the string to create a crossing turn.

Using a quick release

A quick-release legrope attaches to the shin rather than the ankle, and can be easily released if the legrope snags underwater. Pull on the yellow loop and the plug will come away from the strap.

4 Pull the end out of the plug so that you have two loops of string through which to pass the railsaver.

2 Pass the two loose ends back through the turn to form an overhand knot. You should now have a complete loop that can be threaded into the legrope plug.

3 Thread the loop of string through the legrope plug, which should be located on the deck of the board, towards the tail.

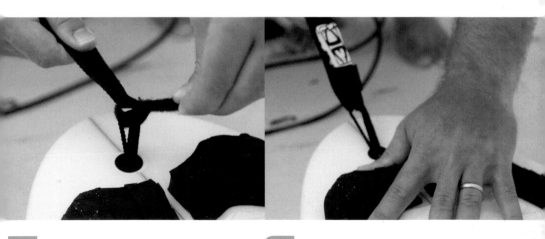

5 Slip the railsaver through both loops of string, then fasten the velcro strap.

6 Hold your board and pull on the legrope with your other hand to ensure everything is secured tightly. Strap the loose end of the legrope to your ankle.

go get started

coming up...

On the beach: 64–75

It's useful to develop your wave sense and get a feel for how to manoeuvre the board before you try to catch your first wave. Practise bodysurfing, paddling, standing up, and manoeuvring your board on the beach. Learning these basics will greatly increase your enjoyment once you do hit the surf.

Into the water: 76–89

Mastering the basic skills of wave-riding will lay the foundation for your surfing development. Learn to find and catch waves, stand and ride the unbroken wave, and move on the wave.

Safety tips: 90–97

Catching a wave and moving on the face is only half the surfing journey – you also need to know how to end your ride and wipe out safely. Learn about surf rescue and reading the waves to make your surfing experience safe and enjoyable.

bodysurfing

The quickest way to enjoy the sensation of surfing is to practise its most basic form – bodysurfing. This is the original and purest type of surfing, and if you're learning to stand up on a board, it offers a fun way to learn some of the most important basic elements that underpin the sport.

You will learn and begin to appreciate how waves break (the motion, rhythm, and feel of the surf zone), and how to spot a wave that can be ridden. With further practice you will to be able to control your direction when you've caught a wave, and will become comfortable with being tumbled in the rolling surf and holding your breath. Each of these aspects are collectively termed "wave sense" – after a time it will become instinct, but the sooner you start developing it the better.

1 How to bodysurf

Find a gentle beachbreak, stand in waist-deep water, and wait until the wave is almost upon you. Then dive forward with your arms above your head – imagine a cartoon superhero flying through the air.

WATCH IT
see DVD chapter 2

2 Make your body as stiff and streamlined as possible, and try and harness the gliding motion, even for a few metres. As you grow more confident, try moving as you bodysurf – a slight lean to the left or right will alter your direction.

Bodysurfing safety

Although bodysurfing is a relatively safe activity, be sure to consider the following safety points:

• Start bodysurfing in a designated swimming area where lifeguards are on duty.

• Being thrown onto shallow sandbars by dumping waves can cause neck and spinal injuries. At first you should avoid waves that are too big or powerful.

• Be sure to bodysurf away from boardriders and only over a sandy bottom, free of reef and rocks.

• If you get dumped, wrap your arms around your head, go with the turbulence, and relax to conserve oxygen. Push off the bottom once you feel the worst of the turbulence has passed. Watch for the next wave and other surfers when you surface.

• As you grow more confident, try wearing flippers or swim fins. Start further out and swim into waves as they break, hugging the wave face by taking off diagonally. You want to angle down the wave face, away from the pitching lip, to avoid being catapulted.

paddling in flat water

Paddling a surfboard in flat water is a good way to experience how the board behaves in water. While bodysurfing offers a taste of the thrills to come, paddling offers a glimpse of the hard graft that makes it all possible. It's also a useful way of finding your "sweet spot" on the board – a balanced position that's ideal for paddling.

Learning to paddle

An important skill in its own right, paddling is the most basic form of surfboard control. In your surfing life you'll spend a great deal longer paddling than you will standing up and riding.

Cup your hands
For the most powerful stroke, keep your hands cupped and your fingers slightly apart.

1 Pulling power
Practise reaching out as far as you can with each stroke. Dig deep and pull hard through the water. To steer, simply pull harder on one side than the other.

2 Paddle with your whole body, not just your arms. Go for long, slow, deep strokes, rather than quick, short, shallow ones. Relax your back and shoulders, to reduce fatigue.

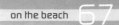

WATCH IT
see DVD chapter 2

Balanced position on board

Start in flat water and get used to balancing comfortably in the prone position. Find your sweet spot – a comfortable balance point where the nose of your board sits just above the surface of the water. Mark this spot with wax on your board, so you will know where to lie. When paddling, feel your abdomen pressed flat against the deck of your surfboard. Activate your abdominal muscles, so you feel as though you are paddling with your whole body.

Body too far back

If your body is too far back (the most common beginner's mistake) the nose of your board will point skywards. You'll find it hard to make forward progress and control your direction.

Body too far forward

If your body is positioned too far forward on the board you will nosedive. The nose of the board will sink under the water and you're likely to fall off.

meet your feet

Take some time to get better acquainted with the soles of your feet. These remarkable devices are the connection between you and your surfboard, and will act as your steering mechanism, accelerator, and brake. You also need to work out whether you are a "natural" or "goofy" footer.

When riding a wave, surfers constantly make tiny shifts in weight distribution, responding to the changing nature of the wave face. In general, the back foot is used to power the turn by pushing down the tail of the board, and is used as a brake, while the front foot acts as the accelerator foot and helps steer the board through a turn.

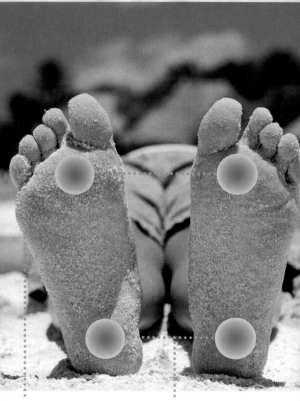

Controlling the board
Control of your surfboard is achieved by shifting your weight between four points – the ball and heel of each foot. Practise spreading your weight evenly between these points and then shifting on and off each of them. Sit down and massage the soles of your feet, then practise spreading your weight again. See if you can feel greater sensitivity in your feet, and how your weight shifts subtly between these four points.

Steering from the balls of your feet
The balls of your feet are used for forehand turns, to turn your board in the direction you are facing.

Steering from your heels
The heels are used for backhand turns, to turn the board away from the direction you are facing.

Are you natural or goofy?

Working out whether you ride natural or goofy is a fundamental part of finding your stance.

- If you aren't sure whether you're a natural or goofy footer, ask someone to give you a gentle push forward from behind when you're standing in a normal, relaxed stance. The foot you instinctively put forward to steady yourself will be your front foot on a surfboard.

- A natural footer on a right-breaking wave faces the wave (riding on their "forehand") and a goofy footer on the same wave will have their back to it (riding on their "backhand"). The opposite applies on left-breaking waves.

Riding natural
When standing on a surfboard, if you put your left foot forward, you are a natural footer (also known as a "regular" footer).

Riding goofy
If you put your right foot forward, you are a goofy footer. A tiny percentage of surfers are switchfoots, and can ride either regular or goofy.

Inside and outside rail

Surfers often refer to moving their weight over the inside or outside rail during a turn. The inside rail is always the rail closest to the wave, and cuts through the water as you trim, while the outside rail is the one closest to the beach.

WATCH IT
see DVD chapter 2

finding your stance

To surf well you need to find a comfortable way of standing on your board. A good stance allows a surfer to control the board's speed and direction, and to translate the mind's intentions into relaxed, flowing movements in response to the constantly changing terrain of a breaking wave.

Setting your position on the board
Your first beach lesson will include pointers for finding your stance:

- Your feet should be across the centre of the board, angled slightly forward – the front foot at about 80° from the centre-line, the back foot at around 85°.

- Bend at the knees and drop your weight into your lower body.

- Crouch slightly forward, with your feet well planted on the deck of the board. Try to make your lower body feel solid and strong while letting your upper body stay relaxed and flexible.

- Hold your front arm up to around chest height and stretch it out in line with your shoulders. This will help you balance, and focus on the direction you are travelling in.

- Your back arm should be bent and held out in front of your face at around chin height.

Anatomy of the stance

How you stand when the board is moving fast over water will differ from how you stand in your first beach lesson. On the water, the body is in constant motion, adjusting and compensating all the time. But learning an idealised stance to begin with gives you a good position to aim for when you start riding.

WATCH IT
see DVD chapter 2

Raise your arms
Keep the arms up when possible. They should be relaxed enough to steady you, but not swinging wildly.

Bend your knees
Keep your knees bent, and think of them as shock absorbers that allow the upper body to stay loose.

Plant your feet
Your feet will need to be in the same place every time, so once you find the correct stance, mark where they go using wax.

Practising your stance

Check out your stance in a mirror or invite feedback from others. This is great practice for getting it right in the surf.

• Adopt your stance as normal, with your feet planted in position on the board, knees bent, and arms raised.

• Ask someone to try pushing you off balance by giving you a gentle shove in the chest, the back, and then shoulders.

• Yield to the push in your upper body by staying loose, using your arms to balance, while staying planted in the lower body.

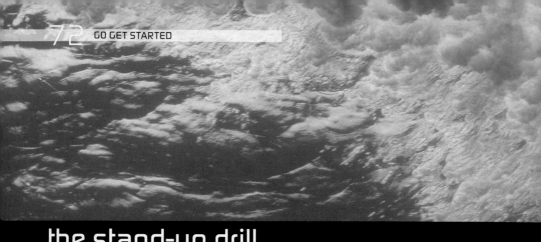

the stand-up drill

Practising on dry land is an important way for you to get familiar with both your board, and some of the basic moves of surfing. Most important of these basic moves is learning to stand up quickly, which is crucial to a successful take off once you hit the waves. Lay your board on the sand, lie down on it, and practise pushing up and getting to your feet in a clean, smooth, swinging motion.

1 Getting to your feet
Place your hands on the rails of the board, level with your chest, then push up with your arms and lift your chest.

2
Move what will be your back foot up to your front knee. Push up with your hands and your back foot, lift your hips, and swing your legs in underneath you.

Practising the stand-up drill

The key to standing up in one fluid movement is placing your hands and feet securely before you spring up. You can practise the drill almost anywhere with room to lie down. Keep repeating the action until it feels easy and natural – you'll find it useful when you start trying it in the water.

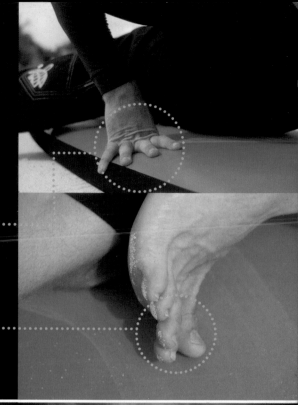

Hands ···
Evenly distribute your weight with your hands. This will stop you from overbalancing.

Feet ···
Place your back foot next to your front knee. This will make it easier to push up to the standing position.

WATCH IT
see DVD chapter 2

3 Plant your front foot in the position you marked with wax. Your feet should be across the centre of the board with your leading foot placed between your hands.

4 Crouch and spread your arms out at shoulder height to balance yourself. Your pose should be close to the ideal stance (see pages 70–71).

Before you hit the waves it's useful to practise how to control your board on dry land. These exercises will help you get you and your surfboard out through breaking waves more easily, and get you used to the shifts in weight required to ride waves.

1 **Steering your board drill**
Find a flat part of the beach and build a small mound of sand. Place your board on top of it, like a see-saw.

board control

The more comfortable you become with manoeuvring your board on land, the less time and energy you will waste once you get into the water, and the more time you will spend surfing.

1 **Manoeuvring your board drill**
Try standing on your board while it is on the mound of sand, and practise maintaining the board in a comfortable balance point.

2 Kneel next to your board. Using your hands, get used to the feel of putting weight on the tail, lifting the nose, and pivoting the board back and forth.

3 Always keep your board perpendicular to the beach and the waves. When you come to wade out through the surf, you'll push down on the tail to lift the nose in order to get the board over approaching waves, then push it back down and continue on your way.

WATCH IT
see DVD chapter 2

2 Try shifting your weight forward, tipping the nose of the board down, as you will when taking off on a wave. Shifting your weight forward will make your board accelerate on a wave.

3 Now practise shifting your weight backwards to make the nose lift. Try and make this a gentle transition rather than a sudden lift. This will make the board decelerate, or lose speed, on a wave.

Now it's time to hit the waves. Make sure there is a competent surfer nearby to watch and help you. Before you enter the water, check that your board is waxed on the deck. Then, put your leash on – just above the ankle on your back foot. Remember, the back foot for natural footers is the right, the left for goofy footers.

catching your first wave

1
Catching whitewater waves
Wade into waist-deep water. Always keep the board perpendicular to the beach and the oncoming waves, and always off to one side or behind you.

2
To get your board through the small whitewater waves, push down on the tail and lift the nose, as you practised on land (see pages 74–75).

3
Wade out as far as you feel comfortable, swing the board around and point it towards shore, keeping it perpendicular to the wave.

Points to remember

- It doesn't matter if your first few rides are short and you end up falling off.

- Don't be in a hurry to stand up. It will take time, but it will be worth the wait.

- Get used to the feeling of being pushed along by a wave.

- If you are struggling to catch a wave, ask an experienced surfer to help by pushing you as the wave approaches.

WATCH IT
see DVD chapter 2

4 Try jumping onto your board as a whitewater wave approaches – your forward momentum should be enough to catch it. When you are in the sweet spot and balanced on your board, paddle strongly until you feel the wave pick you up and push you shorewards.

standing up

As you grow more confident catching waves in the whitewater, sooner or later you will be tempted to try standing up. Your board will feel extremely unstable at first, even if you've put in lots of practice jumping to your feet on land. Most early attempts end in a wipeout, but each time you try, you're learning more about the fundamental transition that will make you a surfer. So keep working at it, and learn to enjoy the wipeouts – there'll be plenty more throughout your surfing career!

At this stage, stay in the whitewater but head further out to get longer rides – it will give you more time and distance in which to try getting to your feet.

1 Standing up in whitewater
To paddle through small waves, push up with your arms and let the wave roll between you and the board. When you are far enough out, turn your board towards the shore.

2 As a wave approaches, start paddling hard. By now you should be used to the feeling of the whitewater hitting you from behind. Hold onto the rails when the wave hits you.

3 Remember the stand-up drill (see pages 72–73). Once you've caught a wave, push up with both arms, both hands firmly gripping the rails below your chest.

Have patience

The simple exercise of paddling out, catching broken whitewater waves, and getting to your feet could easily occupy the first few months or more of your surfing life. Don't despair. This is normal. The more often you can go surfing, the quicker you will advance.

4 Spring up by lifting your hips, pushing up with your arms, and swinging your feet in under you. If you only get to your knees, or one foot and one knee, don't worry – that's allowed. Keep hold of the rails in a low squat if it helps you to balance.

5 Don't be in a hurry to get to a fully erect stance. Use your arms to balance, and if you feel yourself losing your balance, try crouching down lower.

WATCH IT
see DVD chapter 2

punching through the waves

To make it past the advancing waves to the line-up, you will need to duck dive, or turn turtle.

Duck diving involves submerging both your board and body to pass smoothly under the turbulent water of a broken or breaking wave, but can only be done on a shortboard. Turning turtle is a simpler method of passing beneath the waves, and can be practised on a longboard.

Keep paddling
Whether your duck dives are succeeding or not, always start paddling towards the next wave as soon as the previous one has passed over you or released you. This will gain you important ground before the next wave hits you – they don't stop coming and each one will try to push you back towards the shore. So in order to penetrate the whitewater zone and make it to the line-up, you need to have one thing in your mind – keep paddling!

1
Duck diving
When confronted by a broken wave, your instinct may be to push your board away. Instead, push up with your arms and plunge the board under the water.

2
Firmly plant your back foot or knee onto the tail of the board and push as deep and as hard as you can, with the combined force of your hands on the rails and your knee.

3
Timing is everything here. You want to dive as deep as you can, and as close to the oncoming wave as possible, to get under the wave's turbulence.

Turning turtle

To turn turtle, slide off your board as the wave approaches, keeping your hands on the rail. Turn the board over and sink underwater pulling down on the nose to stop it from catching the whitewater. The wave will roll over you and your board. Once it has passed, turn the board over again, climb on, and start paddling.

4 As you reach as deep as you're going to go, start to push the board out in front of you horizontally. As the wave passes overhead, push the nose of the board back up towards the surface.

5 The board's natural buoyancy will help pop you up on the other side of the wave. Lay back down on your board and resume paddling as quickly as possible.

WATCH IT
see DVD chapter 3

sitting on your board

When you make it past the point where the waves are breaking, you'll notice how much quieter and calmer it is. Instead of endless walls of rushing whitewater pushing you shorewards, there will be smooth swells undulating beneath you and other surfers sitting on their boards, chatting and paddling about. Welcome to the line-up.

First you will want to try sitting up on your board, but before you do, paddle a little further out than the other surfers to ensure two things: that you don't get hit by any of the larger waves coming in (the bigger they are, the further out they break); and to give yourself some space to practise sitting up.

WATCH IT
see DVD chapter 3

Manoeuvring your board

It is important to learn how to move your board from a seated position. Lean back while holding on to the rail with one hand, and back-paddle with the other by pushing your hand through the water from the tail of the board towards the nose. Your board will turn to the side your are paddling from. You can also try moving your feet in an egg-beater motion – if both legs spin clockwise, the board will move in that direction.

1 Moving into a sitting position

From the lying position, push up with your arms and swing your legs either side of your board, straddling it between your knees. Grip the rails firmly and evenly for balance. Be careful as at first your board may shoot out from between your legs.

2

Try to keep your back straight and eyes towards the horizon looking for waves. Experiment by gently shifting your weight on the board until you find the most comfortable, stable position. You can take your hands off the rail once you have found this balance point.

finding and catching a wave

Whether in or out of the water, spend time watching waves, and carefully observing how they break. Familiarity with the dynamics of waves is the key to catching and riding them. Watch experienced surfers, too – see which waves they take, and which they let pass. Soon you will learn to differentiate good waves from bad, which will help when you're sitting in the line-up, preparing to catch your first unbroken wave.

Judging and catching waves is a real art. Timing is everything. You should adopt a comfortable paddling position, but even so, at first you may find yourself nose-diving on take-off, or missing waves because of slow paddling. When you sense you are in the right spot to catch a wave, put your head down and paddle hard. You may misjudge a few take-offs, and end up cartwheeling down the face, but keep at it. Eventually, you will catch a wave right on the crest. Take a couple of extra strokes to make sure you have caught the wave. If you get to your feet too soon, you might fall off the back of the wave.

1 Catching an unbroken wave
Watch the horizon while sitting on your board. You'll notice that it wobbles. The bumps are approaching waves and indicate how big they might be.

2
Look for a small- to medium-sized wave. When you see one you can catch, hold the rails of your board, carefully resume the lying position, and start paddling – hard.

3
As the wave nears, look for the peak. This is where it will break first. Paddle yourself into position so that you can take off as close to the peak as possible.

Points to remember

There is a lot to think about when waiting for your wave, but try to remember the following points:

- When you are learning, look for small, gentle waves that peel in one direction.

- Paddle in too early, and the wave may break on top of you. Paddle in too late, and the wave may roll away without you.

- Remember that the rider nearest the breaking part of the wave has right of way. Give them space and never drop in.

- If there are surfers inside the impact zone, paddling back out to the line-up, steer well clear of them.

WATCH IT
see DVD chapter 3

4 Turn your board shorewards. Angle it in the direction that the wave is breaking. On right-handers, angle your board to the right, on left-handers, angle it to the left.

5 Start paddling hard. You'll feel the wave lifting your tail, and your nose begin to point downwards.

6 Continue paddling as the wave lifts you, keeping your body stiff and weighted forward. Match the wave's speed until gravity takes you down the slope.

Riding your first unbroken wave is one of the most magical moments in your surfing career. For the first time you'll feel the sensation that gets so many people hooked – somewhere between skating and flying on a magic carpet.

1 Taking off and riding the unbroken wave
Having caught a wave, prepare to push up to your feet. You don't have to push up as high as you do on broken waves, because the height of the wave means that the board drops down the face.

riding the unbroken wave

Like every other stage so far, it takes time to master and you'll have plenty of wipeouts. Just keep at it. When you get it right, everything happens quickly and easily, and you'll find yourself standing upright, hurtling down the face of the wave.

WATCH IT
see DVD chapter 3

4 Centre yourself over your board with your arms, look forward in the direction that you are travelling, and crouch slightly as you accelerate down the wave face.

2 You need to be quick. Hesitation is your worst enemy. Plant your feet over the centre line and try to angle diagonally down the face so you don't have to turn sharply at the bottom of the wave.

3 Keep your focus directed forwards and avoid leaning back – a common error that puts you at odds with the forward momentum of the wave, and usually results in a fall or missed wave.

5 Lean into the wave slightly, on the balls of your feet if on your forehand, or on the heels if on your backhand. Feel your inside rail run through the water as you near the bottom of the wave.

6 Crouching down slightly will drop your weight into your lower body and lower your centre of gravity, giving you a more stable stance. Try to stay loose and relaxed – if you tense up you're more likely to fall.

moving on the waves

You will soon find yourself riding on the face of the wave, moving fast and feeling in control. Enjoy the sensation of feeling and responding to the wave's subtle changes by leaning, crouching, or adjusting your weight distribution. This is trimming, the most basic wave-riding skill, and it forms the foundation of good technique and style.

1 Trimming across the waves

Angle across the wave, making subtle shifts in your weight distribution to keep your board planing evenly across the face. You may have to crouch slightly, or lean forwards or back to keep your balance, as the wave's shape and speed varies.

Balancing opposing forces

By climbing and dropping you are learning to play with the opposing forces at work in surfing – the force of gravity, and the force of water rushing up the wave face. When in trim these forces are balanced; when you turn up or down the wave, one or other of the forces takes over.

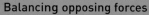

Water flow   Gravity

4 As you approach the top of the wave,

release the inside rail and you'll begin to angle back down the wave. Practise these small but important turns, learning just how far you can push them.

WATCH IT
see DVD chapter 3

2 As you trim across the wave, experiment with shifting your weight from the inside to the outside rail. Lean gently on the balls of your feet and then on your heels. Almost magically, you'll find yourself rising up and down the wave face.

3 As you feel the rhythm of the wave, move more confidently with it. Lean into the wave and you'll feel the inside rail grab as you begin to angle up the wave face.

5 Maintain your speed and momentum but make sure your movements are controlled. Go too fast and you'll either ride over the top of the wave, or drop down into the flats in front of the wave and lose speed.

6 As you get more comfortable with the rhythm, start to crouch into your turn off the bottom, and extend through your legs off the top. You will find this is an effective way to generate more speed as you climb and drop across the wave.

ending your ride

A ride can end in a number of different ways. You may find yourself cruising off the shoulder of the wave into flat water, the wave might simply peter out, or you may fall off, straighten out, or jump off the back.

a b

Straightening out in whitewater
Sometimes you will choose – or be forced – to straighten out in the whitewater and head towards the beach. If you can, carefully resume a lying position as your surfboard loses its speed. If this is not possible, jump or dive off with a shallow trajectory.

Riding off the shoulder
If you get to the end of your ride under control and still upright, try to flow gently off the shoulder of the wave. At first you will probably fall or dive off as momentum disappears, but eventually you'll get the hang of grabbing your rails and crouching down in the prone position in one smooth motion.

WATCH IT
see DVD chapter 3

Finishing safely

Always avoid kicking your board out wildly at the end of the ride, no matter how excited or overwhelmed you feel. A flying surfboard is a dangerous missile for you and other surfers.

c d

c **Cruising over the wave**

If you can see that a wave is about to close out ahead of you, it is preferable to try and pull off the back of the wave before it does so. Simply aim high on the wave and allow your board to cruise over the lip.

d **Jumping over the wave**

Sometimes the wave might close out ahead of you or you may catch a rail when high up on the face. In these situations, you can try to fall or jump over the back of the wave. This has the advantage of keeping you outside the impact zone, saving you the effort of paddling and duck diving back to the line-up.

wiping out safely

Wiping out is the penalty surfers pay for the great pleasures that wave-riding offers, and the sooner you become comfortable with it, the better. It is often a very violent experience, continually reminding you that the sea can be a brutal, merciless medium. But always remember that the keys to dealing with wipeouts are control, calmness, and the knowledge you accumulate with experience.

Wiping out safely
Always try to fall off the side or the back of the board so that it doesn't hit you. When you surface watch out for other surfers, oncoming waves, and your board.

How not to wipe out
Try to avoid kicking your board away too strongly when you wipe out. You don't want your board to hit other surfers or rebound at the end of the legrope and hit you.

Wipeout tips

There are many ways surfers come to grief, from a mis-timed take-off or duck dive, to a snagged rail or over-powered turn, choosing a wrong line on the wave face, hitting a bump or a section that closes out, or simply losing your balance while riding. After the event, you may find yourself separated from your surfboard – legropes can break, velcro can come undone, or the string that ties your legrope to your board may break or come undone. Bear the following tips in mind:

• Assess the situation. Where is your board? Are there any hazards in the area?

• If by chance your board is drifting out to sea, don't swim after it. Ask a more experienced surfer for help, or borrow a board to paddle after it.

• Your instinct may be to swim out of the impact zone towards the calm water of the channel. Don't. Let the whitewater carry you back to shore.

• You may find yourself drifting out to sea in a rip or current. Swim into the whitewater and let it push you shorewards.

WATCH IT
see DVD chapter 3

surf rescue

One day, you may find yourself in the proximity of someone in trouble in the surf and the only one in a position to help – alternatively, you may get into trouble yourself. Having a clear understanding of what to do could help you to keep the situation under control.

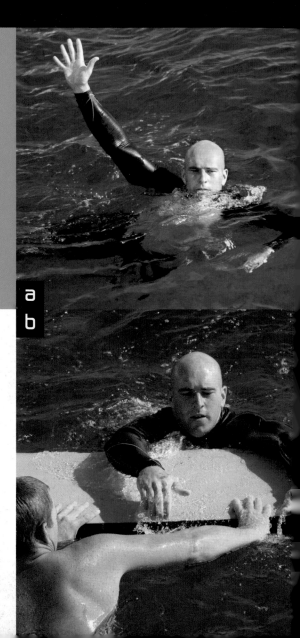

a
b

a Attracting attention
The universal signal for attracting attention is to wave one arm in the air. This can be used if you get into trouble yourself, or need to signal for assistance while you wait with a stricken surfer.

b Holding on
Let the surfer hold on to your board and catch their breath, then reassure them. Don't let a panicked swimmer grab hold of you and pull you under – if necessary give them your board as a buoyancy aid, and tread water calmly next to them.

c Getting to shore
If you think it is necessary, roll the surfer onto your board in front of you, lay behind them and paddle to the beach.

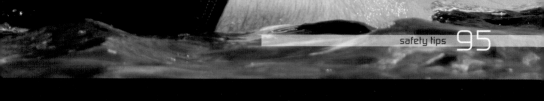

C

If you need rescuing

If you find yourself separated from your board or in touble, the most important thing is to remain calm. Panicking will only lead to bad decisions and a loss of valuable energy.

• Wave one arm in the air above your head, to signal you need help.

• If you've lost your board, tread water and try to stay calm. Panic will only waste energy.

• Swim across rips and currents and into the surf break to get washed back to the shore.

• If you've snapped your board, try and hang on to half of it for flotation but be careful not to cut yourself on jagged fibreglass.

• Other surfers or lifeguards should spot you and come to your aid. For this reason, never surf alone.

WATCH IT
see DVD chapter 3 >

reading the waves

Don't underestimate the importance of spending time simply sitting and watching the waves. Experienced surfers notice a thousand subtleties in a few minutes of scanning the ocean – for example, how the wind is affecting the surface of the waves, what the tide is doing, where the waves are breaking, where the currents are, what hazards might be present, where surfers are picking off the best rides, and where to enter and exit the surf.

Never enter the ocean unless you've studied the prevailing conditions and are confident you can deal with them. For example, is the tide coming in or going out? In some places tides are huge, so you should note where the tide is when you enter the water. Pay particular attention if the tide is incoming as at a certain stage the beach may disappear. In these situations, make sure you are out of the water while there is still some beach, to avoid having to climb in over rocks, up cliffs, or worse!

Watch where waves break
Notice where the waves are breaking and where any rips, currents or channels appear to be. The waves are actually an incredibly accurate map of the sea floor, indicating ocean-depth where they break. Are there deeper sections where the waves aren't breaking? You want to paddle out in the deep-water channels, then angle into the break when you're ready to try and catch waves.

Observe the sets
Waves usually come in sets. Between sets there are sometimes long lulls when the ocean appears to be flat or the waves seem small. Observe how far apart the sets are – are they coming in every ten minutes, or more frequently? It's worth knowing, to avoid being surprised by the size once you have entered the water.

Note how waves break
How are the waves breaking? Are they breaking hard, dumping on the shallows, or are they crumbly and weak? How is the wind affecting them – is it blowing onshore, offshore, or sideshore? This will affect the quality of the waves you will be catching.

go surf

coming up...

Essential techniques: 102–105

Mastering your take offs and surfing with speed and control – these are the keys to developing your surfing. Together they will allow you to catch bigger and better waves and ride them with confidence.

Bottom turns: 106–109

Being able to confidently turn your board back up towards the crest of the wave – the power source – is the foundation of your surfing technique. A sure-footed bottom turn will set you up for more complex manoeuvres throughout your ride.

Top turns: 110–119

Once you reach the top of the wave, what then? Learn how to re-direct your board back down the wave with speed and style.

the take-off

The take-off is the most critical moment of your ride. It is the starting point of all manoeuvres, and begins when the rider stops paddling, pushes up into the standing position, and begins to drop down the wave face.

As you progress you will want to try and catch bigger waves closer to the peak, where the wave is steepest, to generate maximum speed, and therefore the biggest thrills. Here the difference between success and failure is a very fine line indeed.

1 Completing the take-off

The key to a successful take off is commitment. Position yourself to take off right on the apex of the wave. Time your take off precisely – too soon and you'll miss it, too late and you could be thrown into mid-air by the pitching lip.

3

Once you have caught the wave, push up with extra spring, swing your legs quickly into position, and launch yourself into the drop.

2 Paddle strongly and confidently. You can gain extra propulsion by kicking. The earlier you catch the wave, the less vertical, and therefore easier, the take-off will be.

4 Stay centred over your board and avoid leaning back. Be prepared: the board may briefly disconnect from the wave, causing you to literally drop into the curving wave. Be ready to absorb the impact of the drop by bending at the knees and crouching into a smooth bottom turn.

Getting to your feet

As the most important point of the ride, the take-off is the moment when you must know exactly what you want to do; there is no room for extraneous thoughts.

- A confident take-off is going to set you up for the rest of your ride – stay relaxed but aware of what's going on around you.

- You need to be fully focused on the moment, what elite athletes call "in the zone", or yogis call the state of "no mind" – not thinking about anything but what is immediately in front of you.

- You can practise taking off by catching close-out waves. These are hard to ride because everything happens so fast and there's little room for error. Other surfers aren't likely to be riding the close-outs so you should be able to usefully hone your take-off instincts without having to compete for waves.

- Once you make it to the bottom of the close-out wave you can just jump off or straighten out towards the beach.

WATCH IT
see DVD chapter 4

As you become more proficient and ambitious, speed and control will be your greatest allies. When learning to ride a bicycle, you quickly realise that speed adds stability, and the same applies in surfing. Standing on a stationary or slow-moving surfboard is extremely difficult. On a fast-moving surfboard, however, the subtle adjustments of bodyweight needed to keep your balance and steer the board become much easier.

speed and control

1 Surfing with speed and control
To generate more speed, practise riding in the top half of the wave where the face of the wave is steeper. Subtlety angling up and down this vertical part of the wave is a great way to generate speed.

2 Use your leading arm to control your position on the wave, as you tend to go where your front arm is pointing. This arm acts as a mini-surfboard, predicting where your real board will go, the moment before it does.

Speed without control is a dangerous thing. A novice surfer moving fast through a crowded line-up, unable to stop or steer the board, is a serious hazard. Speed and control, therefore, need to grow hand in hand. As you catch bigger waves and experience greater speeds, you need to develop your ability to handle speed, turn, avoid other surfers or obstacles, and ride the waves with the kind of sharp reflexes and presence of mind required in busy surf breaks.

WATCH IT
see DVD chapter 4

3 Generate speed in a comfortable, relaxed posture and keep turning your gaze, arms, and upper body where you want to go.

4 Adopt an easy, relaxed stance, focus on the wave ahead, and be ready and responsive to the changing wave and any obstacles that you encounter. Perfecting your stance in this way is the key to generating speed and improving control.

forehand bottom turn

The bottom turn is often overlooked because there's nothing obviously spectacular about it. But it's the fundamental surfing turn, performed along the bottom of the wave, and it sets you up for whatever moves are to follow. When performed on the forehand, the surfer's face, chest, knees, and toes and are all facing the wave.

1 Performing a forehand bottom turn
On your forehand, since you are facing the wave, lean onto the balls of your feet. The more you lean on the ball of your back foot, the tighter your turn will be.

2 Leaning too hard into a bottom turn will cause the fins to lose grip and spin out. Maintain even distribution of weight both feet at first, with only slightly more on the back foot.

3 Once you feel more confident, start focusing your attention on venturing to the top of the wave. Extend out of your crouched position, straightening your legs as you come out of the turn.

Path of the bottom turn

The bottom turn, whether forehand or backhand, is a smooth u-shaped turn at the base of the wave on your inside rail. It is the transition point where you break free of the downward pull of gravity, and harness the upward force of water rushing up the wave face.

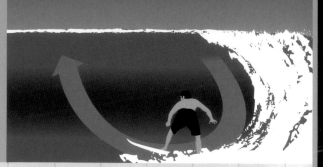

Anatomy of a bottom turn

The bottom turn captures the speed generated from dropping down the wave face, and re-directs it back up the wave so that you have sufficient speed for a smooth top turn or cutback. The goal is to arrive at the top of the wave with plenty of speed.

WATCH IT
see DVD chapter 4

Look in the direction of the turn
Focus on the precise spot that you want to reach at the top of the wave.

Bend your knees
The more you can lower your centre of gravity over your surfboard, the less chance there is of the fins losing grip.

Lean into the turn
Dragging your back hand close to or touching the water will help you lean into the turn.

Move your weight over the inside rail
The more your board is tilted up on the inside rail, the tighter and stronger your bottom turn will be.

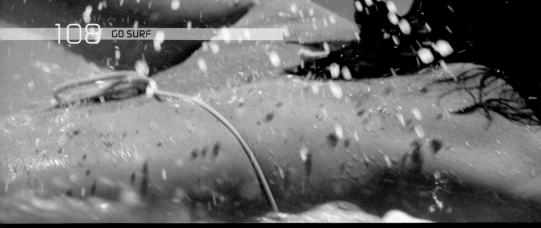

backhand bottom turn

The backhand bottom turn will be more difficult than the forehand version at first because you have your back to the wave, which makes it harder to see what the wave is doing and where you are going.

Instead of leaning onto the balls of your feet as you would for the forehand bottom turn, lean into your heels, look over your leading shoulder, and open your upper body to the direction in which you are moving. Your feet and lower body steer the board while your upper body twists to face the direction you are moving in. Doing quite different things with the upper and lower half of your body at the same time sounds difficult, and it can be at first, like rubbing your tummy and patting your head at the same time, but it is absolutely essential for good surfing and will soon become second nature.

1

Performing a backhand bottom turn

Your lower body needs to be strong and planted in a crouched position. You need to be able to absorb bumps and store speed during the turn, then release that speed as you come out of it.

Hand control

As you become more practised, you will become more aware of your hand positioning during turns. In the backhand bottom turn, for example, it helps to trail your leading hand close to or touching the water behind you as a kind of pivot point in the turn.

2 The lower body performs the turn. To turn, exert pressure on both heels, placing the board on the inside rail. Your upper body should be loose and relaxed in preparation for the next stage.

3 The board will naturally respond to the movement of your body without any strain or struggle, taking you in the direction you want to go in.

WATCH IT
see DVD chapter 4

forehand cutback

The cutback is an important functional manoeuvre that is useful for keeping a surfer near the power-source – the breaking part of the wave.

It is also a means of burning off excess speed and keeping you from out-running the curl. As you become more proficient you'll find there are numerous variations to the type of arc you can draw, but first you need to feel out the dynamics of the basic direction-change.

Path of the cutback
The basic cutback describes an arc from high on the shoulder of the wave, back to the base of the wave, in a clean horseshoe or U-shaped turn. Once the cutback has been completed it can be continued by rebounding off the whitewater at the base of the wave, or leaning into a bottom turn.

WATCH IT
see DVD chapter 4

1 **Performing a forehand cutback**
As soon as you sense a loss of power, angle up high on the wave face and lean on to your outside rail by applying weight to your heels. You should be in a solid, semi-crouched stance.

2 Open your chest and shoulders and turn your head to look back towards the curl. Maintain a constant pressure on your outside rail as the board turns. The more pressure you apply to your back foot, the tighter your turn will be.

3 Your early cutbacks need be little more than a short, clean arc back towards the base of the wave, but you want to aim for a smooth, horseshoe or U-shaped turn that leads you back to the bottom of the wave.

4 At the base of the wave, centre yourself over the middle of your board. Then transfer your weight back to your inside rail to redirect your board along the wave face. Let the whitewater push you towards the wave face for your next bottom turn.

The backhand cutback is actually slightly easier than the forehand cutback because you are facing into the direction of the turn. Again, start high on the shoulder of the wave and draw a clean arc back towards the base of the wave.

Some of your early surfing highlights might involve little more than a couple of successful bottom turns and cutbacks strung together, as you lean from your inside to your outside rail. You should be making smooth transitions between turns, compressing and extending as you go into and come out of each turn.

backhand cutback

1 Performing a backhand cutback
Lean onto the balls of your feet and toes and feel the outside rail grab the wave face. Your knees should be bent, your chest and shoulders open to the direction of the turn, with your arms reaching towards the water.

2 Maintain the arc you started out on by leaning steadily into the turn, looking where you are going. Your trailing arm may even touch the water as a pivot point around which to centre the turn.

WATCH IT
see DVD chapter 4

Leaning into the cutback

The backhand cutback provides a good opportunity to lean hard on the balls of your feet in a turn. The harder you lean, the sharper and quicker the turn. Try crouching lower and closer to the water for a more powerful turn. Learn to recognize how it feels to hold your rail in the water through the turn.

3 The backhand cutback provides you with an early opportunity to lean over heavily into a turn and test your limits. You are out on the shoulder of the wave, so even if you come to grief the wipeout is unlikely to be serious.

4 A simple U-shaped arc should take you to the base of the wave, where you should centre your weight again and be ready to lean into your next bottom turn.

1 Performing a forehand re-entry
Crouch into your bottom turn. Aim high on the wave face with your chest and shoulders opened up towards the top of the wave.

forehand re-entry

A re-entry is a pronounced climb up the face of the wave towards the lip, followed by a sharp turn back down towards the wave's base.

The re-entry allows you to stay close to the curl where the wave is at its steepest, by turning vertically up and down the wave face, rather than moving out on to the shoulder. This allows you to generate maximum speed as you drop back down, or re-enter, the wave.

4 Make the leading arm and your gaze the predictor of the turn – where you point, the turn will follow.

WATCH IT
see DVD chapter 4

2 As you prepare to travel up the wave face and approach the top of the wave, your upper body must lead you through the top turn and prepare for your next move, while your lower body completes the turn.

3 As you near the top of the wave, transfer your weight to your outside rail. Drive the board through the turn by putting more pressure on the back foot, while maintaining the arc until the board is pointing towards the bottom of the wave.

5 Either drop all the way back down the face to the bottom of the wave and into another bottom turn, or check your descent earlier and bring the board into trim mid-face.

Path of the re-entry

The re-entry takes you from the base of the wave, up to the lip, and back down again. This is the basic template for modern high-performance surfing. When you get to the bottom of the wave, aim to get back to the top. When you get to the top, aim for the bottom – the faster and more vertically the better.

Like the backhand cutback, the backhand re-entry can often feel easier than its forehand counterpart, because you are facing the direction of the turn. Remember to allow your upper and lower body to move independently because this turn requires more twisting than any you've done so far.

backhand re-entry

1 **Performing a backhand re-entry**
As you come out of your backhand bottom turn you will have your back to the wave as you travel up the face. Look up to the top of the wave, and as you start moving upwards, release your inside rail and transfer your weight onto the centre line of the board.

2 Open your chest and shoulders and look to the base of the wave, and allow your board to climb the wave face. At the apex of the turn you should achieve separation of the upper and lower body – board pointing to the sky, body swivelled at the waist, and your upper body facing back down the wave.

Re-entry tips

• The more pressure you apply to your back foot, the sharper your turn and more vertical your trajectory will be.

• Maintaining upper and lower body separation is essential. The lower body completes the manoeuvre while the upper body prepares for the next stage of the turn.

3 At the top of the turn, transfer your weight onto the outside rail. Your board will almost magically swing around back under you, helped by gravity and the force of the breaking lip. You will feel almost weightless for an instant as your board swings around almost 180°.

4 As you reach the base of the wave, re-centre your weight, absorb the speed and impact with bent knees, and then lean into your heels for your next bottom turn.

WATCH IT
see DVD chapter 4

the floater

The floater involves riding right over the top of a close-out section and floating back down with the whitewater. This tricky manoeuvre can be useful if the waves are sectioning, and it is fun to try and learn, even for relative beginners.

It's best to attempt the floater on small crumbly waves at first, where the drop is short and the landing gentle. Get the feel for the moment of weightlessness and you'll soon start to feel more confident. Take it easy though – even experienced surfers have broken boards and ankles attempting floaters.

Path of the floater
The floater is similar to an extended re-entry, but instead of riding up to the lip of the wave and turning back down, the surfer rides up to the lip, hovers laterally over the whitewater, then drops back down again. See pages 140–141 for an advanced version of the floater.

WATCH IT
see DVD chapter 4

1 Performing a floater

If you are suddenly confronted by a close-out section, aim to do a smooth bottom turn as you approach it, projecting up the face as if you're going to do a regular top turn.

2

Instead of turning at the top, just keep going, up and onto the oncoming whitewater section.

3

You'll feel loose and weightless for an instant as you skim over the foam. Staying centred and balanced over your board is key, with your legs spread slightly wider than normal, and your knees slightly bent, ready to absorb the impact of landing.

4

As your fins and gravity take hold, you'll begin to descend. If your timing is right, the lip will land just before you, and a cushion of whitewater will help soften your landing. Give at the knees to absorb the impact and ride out of the whitewater.

go further

coming up...

Longboarding: 124–127

Cross-stepping and nose-riding are two of the great joys of longboarding but they are a lot harder than they look. Learn the essential skills to master these time-honoured technqiues.

Sharpen your turns: 128–135

Sharpening your turns and linking them smoothly together into a cohesive whole is the hallmark of good surfing. Learn how to surf with greater speed and commitment to get the most from your surfing.

Advanced techniques: 136–143

Tube riding, aerials, advanced floaters and bigger waves – these are some of the big thrills of the wave-riding experience. But they don't come easily. When you're ready, these tips will fast-track your development.

Surfing horizons: 144–149

Surfing will take over your life if you let it and the wonderful thing is, it can be all things to all people – exotic travel, big-wave adventure, elite competition, simple fun. Work out what path your surfing journey will take.

walking the board

If shortboards aren't your thing, or if you've mastered trimming and can nurse your longboard through a few turns, it's time to start walking the board. Even if you enjoy shortboarding, don't forget that you can have lots of fun on small-wave days by riding a longboard. Longboards can catch tiny waves and go fast on the smallest peelers. This is where the longboard comes into its own.

There are two reasons why a surfer is able to walk the board without nose-diving. One is that the curl of the breaking wave anchors the tail, acting as a counter-balance to the surfer standing on the nose. The other is the upward flow of water on the wave face gathering against the bottom of the nose of the board, which acts as a supporting cushion.

1 Cross-stepping on the board
You are trimming along a wave, sensing you need to move your weight forward to maintain your momentum. This is an ideal point to try cross-stepping.

2 Instead of shuffling tentatively towards the nose, put your weight on your front foot. Lift your back foot cleanly over it and take a short step forwards, so that your legs are crossed.

WATCH IT
see DVD chapter 5

Cross-stepping tips

• Standard legropes can easily become entangled during cross-stepping, due to the repeated step-overs it requires. It is simplest not to wear one, but if you must wear a legrope, use a special longboard version that fastens around your shin or knee.

• Make your cross-steps quick, light, and smooth, and don't lift your feet too high. Longboarding is all about style, so try to make it relaxed and casual.

3 Put the weight on your new front foot, lift your new back foot and swing it forward in the same way, so that you end up in your normal stance again – just closer to the nose.

4 You can repeat this process until you reach the nose of your board, but be careful not to go too far and nose-dive into the wave.

One of the great joys of longboarding is the nose-ride. It is graceful, stylish, and above all, seems to defy the obvious laws of physics.

The sensation of gliding along a wave with no surfboard in front of you is almost like flying. At first, you might only stay on the nose for an instant, before cross-stepping back to the tail. As you become more confident, your nose-rides will become longer and more graceful. The crowning moment of a nose-ride is to hang five or hang ten – planting one or both feet on the nose of the board.

riding on the nose

Nose-riding tips

Before you move foward on the board, you need to anchor the tail in the curl of the wave and make sure the inside rail is neatly locked into the wave face:

- Angle the board across and down the wave to set your inside rail onto the wave face.

- As you step forward from the back end of the board, the tail will begin to lift.

- You should be able to feel the board either grabbing under the curl, or lifting too high, in which case you need to retreat back to the tail again to avoid nose-diving.

- Large, heavy longboards with a single, long-raked fin and a concave section under the nose are best for nose-riding.

WATCH IT
see DVD chapter 5

Anatomy of a nose-ride

Nose-riding is a bit like standing on a
see-saw, with you at one end and the
lip or foam of the wave on the other.
It requires you to reach a delicate
equilibrium and sensitivity to the changing
wave face in order to pull it off successfully.

Tail of the board
The tail needs to
be anchored in the
lip or foam as a
counter-balance.

Lean back
Arch your back with
your arms hanging
down behind you, and
lean back. This will
help to shift your
weight towards the
tail even as you are
standing on the nose.

Foot positioning
You can place one
foot (hang five) or
both feet (hang ten)
right on the nose of
the board.

sharpen your bottom turns

Most advanced manoeuvres rely on a precise and sure-footed bottom turn to send you back towards the top of the wave quickly and with all your momentum. The best way to achieve this is simple practice.

Go out and have a specific bottom-turn session – do nothing but take off and concentrate on your bottom turns, both backhand and forehand. This is a great way to approach surfing conditions that only provide limited rides, such as short, peaky beach breaks, or close-out waves.

Another way to improve your technique is to look at photographs in magazines or to watch videos of surfers making bottom turns. The more of the bottom of the surfer's board you can see, and the closer to the water they crouch, the more committed and powerful the turn.

WATCH IT
see DVD chapter 5

1 Making sharper bottom turns
Before you enter the turn, focus on the point at the bottom of the wave where you want to start your bottom turn. This will help you to instinctively lean more heavily into it once you get there.

Bottom turn tips

- Bend at the knees, not the waist, to improve your stability through the turn – a stiff-legged bottom turn will feel awkward and unbalanced.

- Keep your weight over the back foot to drive the turn and help your fins grab.

- The board you use will affect the turn you make. Longer boards draw wider turns, while shorter boards with a steeper rocker will turn more sharply.

2 Drive into and through the turn with power and commitment by throwing your weight over the inside rail. Experiment with the positioning of your feet and arms, and how much you bend your knees. You'll know when you've found the perfect position because your turns will feel smooth and flowing.

3 Begin to extend your legs as you come out of the turn and project up the face, carrying the speed from your bottom turn upwards into your next manoeuvre.

sharpen your cutbacks

The horseshoe, or U-shaped, cutback (see pages 110–113) is really only half a cutback. The ultimate aim of the full cutback is to carve a neat, flowing, figure-of-eight turn, continuing the arc back into the lip or whitewater, and coming out of it in control, ready for your next bottom turn.

Points to remember

• Visualizing the turn can help you to find the flow needed to link the different phases together smoothly.

• Aim to eliminate excess movement or awkward pumping and hopping motions through the turn.

• The hallmark of a good cutback is minimal body movement and a board that travels smoothly through the wave, like a hot knife through butter.

• Common mistakes include catching a rail, losing speed, or being engulfed by whitewater.

1 Making sharper cutbacks
Take a high, fast line near the top of the wave. Leaning into the cutback, put your board onto your outside rail. Your upper half should begin to open to the direction of the turn.

4 With your back to the face of the wave, begin to project up the face towards the lip. Prepare to rebound off the section by turning your upper body back down the wave face, then release your inside rail in preparation for your turn off the foam.

2 Start leaning into your cutback, putting your board onto your outside rail. Keep your knees bent, arms out, and your upper half opening to the direction of the turn.

3 Keep turning and keep opening your shoulders to the direction of the turn. Turn at the waist and focus on the spot on the lip ahead of you that you'll use to rebound off, much like a backhand re-entry.

WATCH IT
see DVD chapter 5

5 Bend your legs to absorb the impact of rebounding off the foam. Focus your attention back to the base of the wave, and stay centred ver your board as it swings back under you with the force of the whitewater.

6 You will experience a magical moment of weightlessness as your board rebounds off the whitewater and you find yourself travelling back down the wave again, this time on your inside rail.

sharpen your re-entries

The measure of a good re-entry is how fast, high, and tightly it is executed. A more advanced re-entry uses the pitching lip of the wave to aid a sudden change of direction.

Coming out of a good re-entry is a bit like launching into a take off all over again, hence the name re-entry. Enjoy the feeling of the moment of weightlessness and don't be discouraged if you find yourself falling more than pulling it off. You'll learn something every time, and be one step closer to mastering the manoeuvre.

1 Making sharper re-entries
As you enter your bottom turn, focus your attention on a precise spot at the top of the wave that you want to hit, as close to the pitching lip as possible.

2
Lean hard onto your inside rail to force a tight bottom turn, and as you do so, keep focusing on the top of the wave. Start to guide your board up towards it.

3
As you reach the top of the wave, your front arm should begin to swing down (predicting the direction of the turn), and your back arm should swing up behind you and above your head, guiding the turn.

Top-turn variations

There are numerous varieties of top turns in addition to the re-entry – the hack, layback, carve, and fins-free – and you will inevitably experiment with them as you progress. Getting the feeling for the fundmental 180° re-entry, and the force of the lip at the top of the turn, will stand you in good stead for a myriad of variations.

WATCH IT
see DVD chapter 5

4 The critical moment is the apex of the turn, as your board collides with the lip. Keep your knees bent in preparation for the shock.

5 The impact as your board hits the lip will naturally swivel your board back down the wave face. Your job is to simply stay over it as it does so, using your arms for balance, your legs for shock absorption, and your torso for rotation.

6 Re-centre your weight over the board as you drop back down the wave and prepare for your next bottom turn.

linking manoeuvres

Breaking each manoeuvre down into stages and learning them separately is important, but ultimately you should be able to string them all together like beads on a thread, with one manoeuvre flowing smoothly into the next.

There are common movements in many surfing manoeuvres. For example, the middle of a full cutback is nothing more than a simple bottom turn. Tube-riding is really just trimming inside the wave.

WATCH IT
see DVD chapter 5

Developing flow and fluidity

Flow and fluidity are the qualities you require, which only stands to reason considering the medium through which you're travelling. This means being sensitive to the most subtle of changes under your feet.

The key is to keep focusing on your next destination on the wave, and when you reach it, to look ahead to the next one. When you reach the bottom of the wave, look to the lip; when you get to the lip, look back to the bottom, and so on as the wave dictates.

Visualization can help you to flow smoothly from one manoeuvre to the next. Sit on the beach and "mind-surf" the waves before you paddle out. See yourself flowing from one turn to the next, your board running smoothly out of one arc and into the next. Then put these images into action.

catching bigger waves

One of the great things about improving your surfing is being able to tackle a wider variety of waves and ocean conditions. It is important to go at your own pace, but one day you'll find yourself in position for a bigger wave than any you've ever ridden before. It will be a personal "moment of truth", a moment when all your surfing groundwork up to that point will be put to the test.

Another great thing about tackling bigger waves is that when you return to smaller surf, you will feel supremely confident and ready to push your surfing harder.

WATCH IT
see DVD chapter 5

Big-wave tips

- Train for the big stuff by building your strength, fitness, and stamina. Bodysurfing and swimming are great for your fitness. If you can hold your breath for long periods and swim long distances in a churning ocean, bigger surf will not intimidate you.

- It's easy to lose your bearings in big surf so find landmarks on the shore to show you where to sit in the line-up. Look at the shoreline and find two stationary points to align yourself with – perhaps a tall tree opposite you on the beach, and a prominent rock, off to one side at the edge of the bay. Position yourself where the two intersect.

- Resist the urge to paddle out to sea to avoid being caught by bigger waves when a set appears, as doing so means you risk missing them altogether.

- When the wave approaches, paddle hard and with confidence. Big waves travel faster than smaller ones, so you need to work hard to get up to speed.

- Once you have made the decision to paddle for a wave – don't hesitate.

- Once you have caught the wave, swing quickly up to your feet.

- Lean into the take-off to help you make the drop, not back into the wave, which will separate you from your board.

riding in the tube

Tube-riding is the big one – the great mystical, transcendental surfing experience, the place where time expands, and many more epithets that entirely fail to describe this most magical of surfing moments. In layman's terms, a surfer gets tubed when they ride inside the curl of a breaking wave.

The secret of tube-riding is timing, positioning, and relaxation. Consider the scenario: you're driving your board through another carving bottom turn, looking ahead to where you want to go, and you realise that the wave appears to be breaking too far in front of you. While your instincts scream at you to either straighten out towards the shore or try and outrun the pitching lip to the safety of the shoulder, the tube ride requires that you lose speed, hold your line, and let the wave break over the top of you.

Riding the tube

- If the wave is tubing ahead of you, go as fast as you can – either by pumping the board, drawing out a long bottom turn or taking a high line on the wave face – to put yourself under the lip as it curls ahead of you.

- If the wave is tubing behind you, do a pronounced stall. Like slamming on the brakes of a car, suddenly putting your weight on your back foot and sinking the tail causes you to lose speed abruptly.

- As the tube curls over you, shift your weight forward and bring the board into trim. The lip will begin to descend over you, and your view of the beach will be obscured. You will be looking out of a spinning, almond-shaped hole.

- Even though you may be surrounded by water, ride the wave almost as normal. Stay centred and balanced over your board and crouch down to fit the dimensions of the tube.

- Keep your front arm out ahead of you, letting it guide you, and stay focused on the light at the end of the tunnel.

- If you aren't going to make it out of the tube, fall off the back of your board into the wave, kicking your board away in front of you. Lie flat and relax, allowing the turbulence to take you.

WATCH IT
see DVD chapter 5

As well as being useful for riding over smaller, close-out waves, the floater can be used in more challenging conditions to negotiate larger waves that are sectioning ahead of you. The drop back down to the wave face is longer, and requires strength and balance to absorb the greater impact of the landing.

advanced floater

Instead of doing a regular top turn, the floater involves hovering up on top of the peeling lip and letting it carry you up and over the section and back down onto the clean face of the wave. This is a tricky and quite advanced manoeuvre, but a great one to have in your repertoire for surfing in fast, peeling waves.

WATCH IT
see DVD chapter 5

Advanced floater tips

- Watch out for an opportunity to try the floater – for example, when a fast, peeling section threatens to race away in front of you.

- Approach the lip with the bottom of your board flat, and position it quite deliberately, over the edge of the lip.

- Stabilize yourself with a wide, centred stance, then prepare to balance and hover on the lip as it peels away, using your arms for balance.

- As you begin to descend back onto the face, brace yourself for the shock and give at the knees to absorb the drop.

- Reconnect with the face of the wave, set your fins and rail, and prepare for your next bottom turn.

- Be warned, the floater is a difficult manoeuvre that can result in a broken board or injury if not executed correctly.

aerials

Surfing is a sport that keeps on evolving as successive generations get their hands on it and put their skills and imagination to work. Aerial manoeuvres have been one of the biggest areas of experimentation in recent years and there are almost endless variations on the theme.

The aerial's closest relative is the re-entry, the chief difference being that you don't turn at the lip and return to the base of the wave. Instead you carry the upward momentum into pure flight. Complex twists and spins (such as the one pictured below) are the preserve of a handful of aerial specialists, but it helps to have something to aim for.

WATCH IT
see DVD chapter 5

Aerial tips

- Focus on the part of the wave you want to reach, such as a close-out section ahead of you that can be used as a launch pad, then as you project towards the lip, try to lift the nose of the board by applying pressure on your back foot.

- Make sure that you build enough speed and carry it through the bottom turn prior to taking off.

- Prepare for the moment of weightlessness by extending upwards and absorbing the flight of the board under you by bending your knees into your chest as you head skywards.

- Place one or both hands on the rail of the board to help control your flight path.

- If you have succeeded in staying over your board, you should be able to direct the board back down with your feet and the help of gravity, with your arms spread for balance.

- Bend your legs to absorb the impact as your board re-connects with the wave. Aim for a point where the upward bounce of foam from the breaking lip can cushion your landing.

competition

If you decide that surfing really is your thing, a great way to hone your skills is to test yourself in the heat of competition. Local contests are also a good way to meet other surfers and be a part of your local surfing community. Professional surf contests are a good opportunity to pick up pointers on your technique by watching the pros in action.

Entering a surf contest

Local surf competitions usually involve 20- to 30-minute heats with two to four surfers competing at once. Surfers are marked out of ten on their best two or three rides. Points are awarded for the length of the ride, the height of the waves, the number of manoeuvres, the degree of difficulty, and style.

Joining a club

Boardriders' clubs can be a useful way of getting to know other surfers and surf spots, both in your local area and further afield. Even if you live a long way from the beach, joining a club will put you in touch with other surfers, making it easier to share travel costs and discover new waves. If there are no boardriders' clubs in your area, why not start one?

Watching the pros

If you really want to see how far wave-riding can be taken, get yourself to a professional surf contest. There are various levels of competition and elite surfers compete in the World Championship Tour, which visits most continents in their prime surf season. Pro surfing's governing body, the Association of Surfing Professionals, webcasts most events live so you can watch them on the internet wherever you are. Go to www.aspworldtour.com for tour details and webcasts.

surf travel

One of the best things about surfing is the endless pursuit of waves. Early on in your surfing career, you may want to try surfing at the next bay along the coast, then as you grow in skills and confidence, perhaps take a trip even further to a wave you've heard about from someone else. And so it will continue, for the rest of your surfing life.

Travel to learn

If you don't live by the beach, surfing in an exotic destination for a couple of weeks is a great way to kick-start your development, or give it a nudge along if you seem to be stagnating.

This map is a handy guide to choosing the right surf destination for you. It lists the best surfing regions along with details of water temperature, crowds, and difficulty. Be sure to pick a destination that suits your level of ability. For example, the North Shore of Oahu, Hawaii during the winter is no place for beginners. Use the internet to plan your trip – it's a great tool for researching destinations, local clubs, and surf conditions (see pages 150–151).

East-coast USA

California, USA

Mexico

Caribbean

Costa Rica

Hawaii

Tahiti

GLOBAL SURF SPOTS
Key

■	Warm water
■	Cold water
●	Beginner
●	Intermediate
●	Advanced
🏃	Low crowds
🏃🏃	Moderate crowds
🏃🏃🏃	High crowds

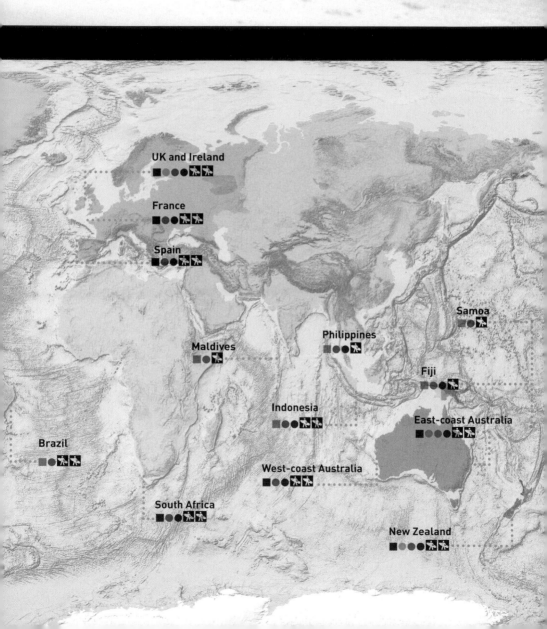

really big waves

One day, you will turn up at the beach and find waves bigger than any you have ever seen. Aside from the fluttering feeling in your stomach, you might be struggling with a simple dilemma: do I paddle out? No-one can answer that for you. All you can do is listen to that inner voice, your instinct. You're unlikely to want to surf in waves over head-height in the first year or two of your surfing career, but if you find yourself thriving on the big stuff, make sure you know your limits and don't jump in over your head.

Vital for big-wave surfing is a high level of fitness, a big-wave board for extra stability, and knowledge of the surf itself (it's important to plan your route to the line-up and back to the shore, and to spot any hazards). If you're serious about riding big waves, work your way up gradually and become accustomed to your bigger board on small-surf days. The actual riding of big waves is not especially difficult – the speed can be greater, the turbulence generated by the high volume of water can be hard to negotiate, but you have more time to make moves, get to your feet, and plot and execute turns.

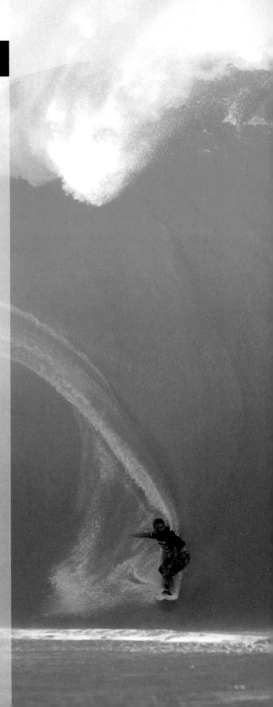

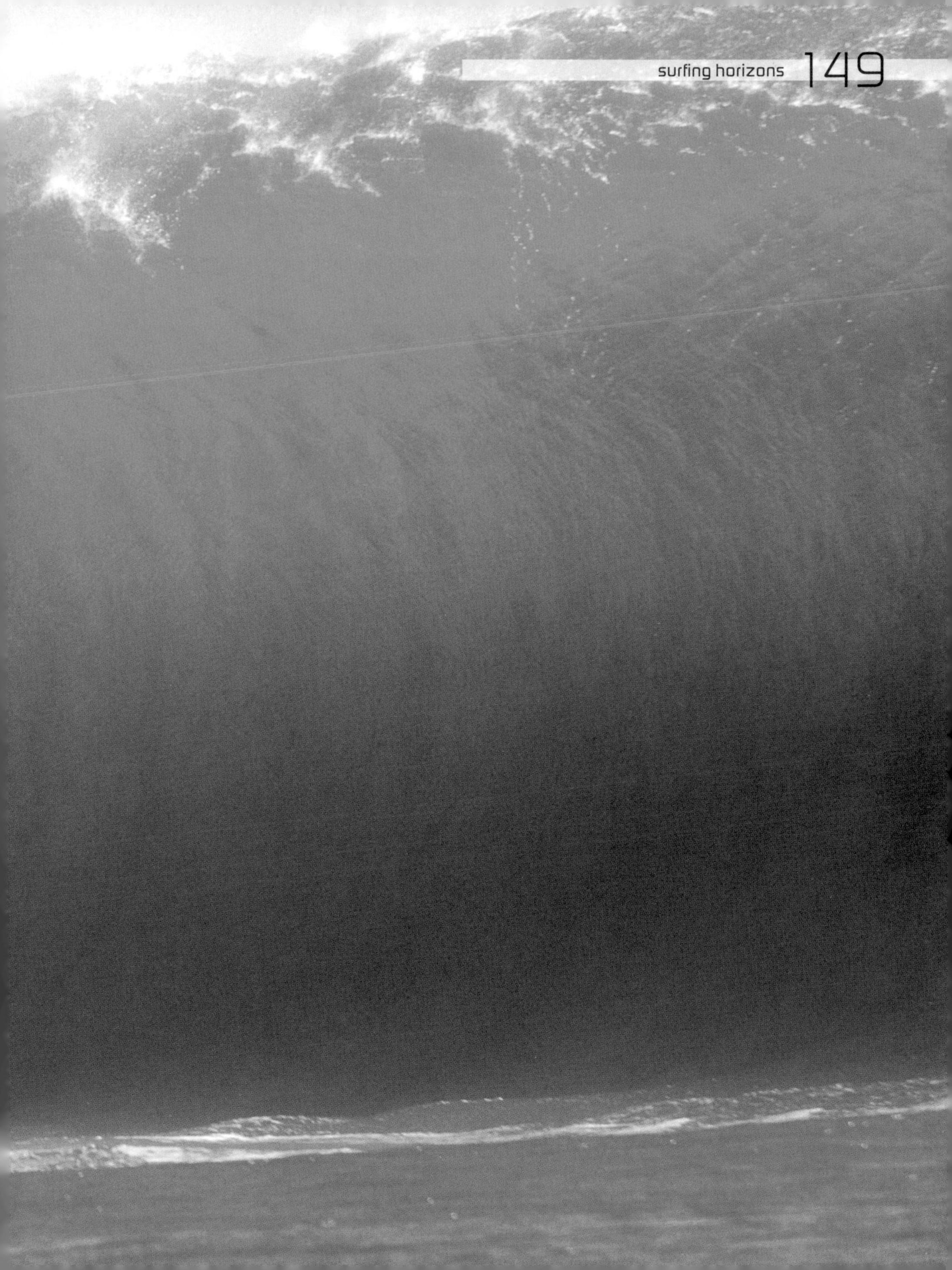

surfing on the web

Listed below is a small selection of surfing websites from around the world, containing everything from national associations, surf travel operators, and environmental organizations, to online magazines, surf-spot listings and information, and weather forecasts.

UK and IRELAND resources

www.britsurf.co.uk
The British Surfing Association is the governing body for surfing in Britain. The site carries information about surf schools, coaching, surf clubs, and the various BSA championships.

www.isasurf.ie
The Irish Surfing Association is the national governing body for surfing in Ireland.

www.sas.org.uk
Surfers Against Sewage is an environmental pressure group.

www.coldswell.com
Coldswell.com forecasts surf, provides swell maps, and weather information for the UK.

AUSTRALIA resources

www.surfingaustralia.com
Surfing Australia is the governing body for surfing in Australia. Its site has details of competitions, camps, surf schools, and clubs.

www.swellnet.com.au
Swellnet is a website that offers daily surf forecasts and news in Australia.

www.cleanocean.org
The Clean Ocean Foundation is an organization that campaigns for greater environmental awareness and respect.

NEW ZEALAND resources

www.surfingnz.co.nz
Surfing's governing body in New Zealand. The site carries surfing news, details about events and competitions, and surfer profiles.

www.surf2surf.com
Surf2Surf is a New Zealand-based surfing guide providing news and forecasts.

INTERNATIONAL resources

www.aspworldtour.com
The Association of Surfing Professionals is the governing body of professional surfing. The website has details of surfers, events, and news.

www.isasurf.org
The International Surfing Association is the world governing authority for surfing, bodyboarding, and all wave-riding activities.

https://www.fnmoc.navy.mil/PUBLIC/WAM/all_glbl.html
Global ocean swell charts from the US Navy's meteorological service, forecasting conditions up to six days in advance.

www.surfaidinternational.org
SurfAid International is a medical charity helping local communities in remote surf regions.

www.wannasurf.com
Wannasurf is a website containing worldwide surf travel information.

surf talk

Aerial – a manoeuvre where the surfer flies into the air and lands back on the wave.

Backhand/backside – riding with your back to the wave.

Banks/sand banks – bottom contours on the sea-bed formed by shifting sand, which influence the shape of a wave.

Beach break – a surf spot where waves break over a sandy stretch of beach, often in a random pattern. Where the waves break is influenced by the location of **sand banks.**

Bodyboard – a small, soft, foam surfcraft used for riding waves in a prone position.

Bodysurf – to ride waves without any form of surfcraft, other than your body.

Bottom turn – a turn across the base of the wave.

Cutback – a manoeuvre where the surfer carves a U-shaped turn on the face of the wave back towards the whitewater (also known as **foam**).

Drop in – to catch a wave that another surfer is already riding. Bad practice.

Duck dive – to push yourself and your board under a breaking wave.

Fins – small, keel-like devices fixed to the bottom of the surfboard to facilitate steering.

Floater – a manoeuvre where the surfer hovers on the breaking whitewater of the wave and drops down to the base of the wave.

Foam - see **whitewater.**

Forehand/frontside – riding with your front to the wave.

Goofy footer – surfer who rides a surfboard with his or her right foot forward.

Impact zone – the area of a surf spot where waves first break.

Left-hander – a wave that peels from right to left, from the perspective of surfers on the wave, or left to right from the perspective of those watching from the beach.

Longboard – a traditional-style long surfboard, 2–3 m (6–10 ft) in length.

Natural footer – surfer who rides a surfboard with his or her left foot forward. Also known as a "regular" footer.

Nose-ride – to stand on the nose of a surfboard while riding a wave.

Off-shore – a wind that blows from the land towards the ocean (favourable for surfing).

On-shore – a wind that blows from the ocean towards the land (unfavourable for surfing).

Peak – the apex of a wave as it begins to crest.

Point break – a surf spot where waves peel at an angle along a headland, or other protruding finger of land.

Rail – the edges of a surfboard. The inside rail is the edge that cuts through the wave when **trimming**, while the outside rail is the edge closest to the beach.

Reef break – a surf spot where waves break over reef.

Re-entry – a manoeuvre where the surfer turns at the apex of the wave and drops back down the wave face.

Right-hander – a wave that peels from left to right, from the perspective of surfers on the wave, or right to left from the perspective of those watching on the beach.

Section – a portion of a breaking wave that breaks ahead of the primary curl line.

Shortboard – the most popular type of board, usually around 2 m (6 ft) in length and generally for small waves.

Shoulder – the unbroken outer edge of a peeling wave.

Side-shore – a wind that blows parallel to the coast (less than ideal for surfing).

Tail – the rear of a surfboard. The tail can be a round, square, pin, diamond, or swallow tail.

Thruster – a surfboard with three fins. The modern standard for shortboards.

Trimming – travelling across the wave face, as opposed to making a turn, by climbing and dropping on the wave.

Whitewater – The broken part of the wave. Also known as the **foam.**

index

thanks to...

Thanks from the author

I'd like to thank Stephanie Farrow, Cameron Craig, Katie Eke, Richard Gilbert, and all at Dorling Kindersley for the opportunity to go surfing in the Maldives for two weeks under the guise of work. To Alex Dick-Read, editor of The Surfer's Path (www.surferspath.com), the cleanest, greenest surf magazine on the planet) – thanks for the sensitive handling of my sometimes garbled prose.

To our surfers, Austin Langridge and Lyndsay Noyes, you were a pleasure to work and surf with – many thanks. To Bruce Lee, Kellie Hughes, Andrew Flitton, Jake Donlen, Bill Sharp, and everyone at Billabong, thanks for your support, the loan of the surfers, and the flash gear. Massive appreciation to Chris Prewitt at Tropicsurf for his skills and wisdom, and his colleagues Jack Chisolm and Ross Phillips. To Team Scubazoo – love your work. To everyone at Four Seasons, Kuda Huraa is my most outlandish surfing fantasies come to life – can't thank you enough.

Mark Lane from Surfing Australia provided invaluable assistance with the surfing theory and tips – these guys are world leaders. And thanks to Chris Garrett for the loan of the beautiful timber veneer board (www.chrisgarrett.shapes.com.au). I'd like to make special mention of all the great surfers who have helped inform my own understanding and enjoyment of surfing over the years – Cheyne Horan (www.cheynehoran.com.au), Robbie Page, Nick and Tom Carroll, Kelly Slater, Andrew Kidman (www.litmus.com.au) and Martin Dunn (www.surfcoach.com). If you ever get the opportunity to learn from any of these masters, seize and cherish it.

And as instructed (and I hope I've got this right) "big props to the wives" for allowing us to disappear surfing every day throughout this elaborate scam/gruelling work assignment.

Enjoy your surfing, share the waves, and keep our oceans clean.

Thanks from Dorling Kindersley

DK would like to thank everybody who worked tirelessly, across several different timezones, to make this book and DVD happen. Thanks to Juliana Ang, Tom, Martin, and the team at Four Seasons Kuda Huraa; to Ross Phillips and Chris Prewitt of Tropicsurf; to Billabong Australia for the loan of Austin Langridge and Lyndsay Noyes; to Austin and Lyndsay for being fantastic; and to Cameron Craig for giving up so much time and paddling to the project. We would also like to thank Bob Bridle for editorial assistance, Sara Oiestad for design assistance, and Margaret McCormack for indexing.

Thanks for the pictures

The publisher would like to thank the following for their kind permission to reproduce their photographs: (Key: a-above; b-below/bottom; c-centre; l-left; r-right; t-top)

Andrew Shield: 30-31b, 97bl, 144br, 145br; Beachbeat Boards: 44-45c; billabongxxl.com: Tim Mc Kenna 148-149; Corbis: Catherine Karnow 23c; Covered Images: Karen Wilson 138-139t; DK Images: Paul Wilkinson 27cla; Getty Images: Uwe Krejci 145tl; Ted Grambeau: 136-137t; Surfing World: Peter Eastway 160; Surfpix: Sean Davey 32, 142bc, 142bl, 142c, 142cl, 142-143br, 142-143cr, 143bc, 143c; Tom Woods 126bl; Wetter Zentrale: 33cr, 33tl

All other images © Dorling Kindersley
For further information see: www.dkimages.com

TROPICSURF *explore, dream, discover*

Your surfing dreams are closer than you think. Tropicsurf Academy is the innovative and exciting place where you can discover secrets and triumphs follow. Offering detailed learning programs via tropical paradises or web-based e-learning, our mission is your ultimate surfing experience. Frustrated beginner eager for fun and progress? Keen to get tubed, nose-ride or tow-in? How about surfing a perfect peeling wave with not a soul in sight? Whatever your level of ability, for anything you can dream of, Tropicsurf has the experts, locations, and experience to deliver the best surfing holiday of your life.

FOUR SEASONS RESORTS
Maldives

Four Seasons Resorts Maldives offers two distinct resorts and the finest catamaran cruise experience. Set amidst a vibrant garden island, the newly rebuilt Four Seasons Resort Maldives at Kuda Huraa is favoured for its magical Maldivian village setting and legendary Four Seasons service. Beach Bungalows with plunge pools and breathtaking ocean views, and supremely luxurious water bungalows, offer endless views of sunrise, sunshine, and sunset. Situated in the remote Baa Atoll, the company's second resort, Four Seasons Resort Maldives at Landaa Giraavaru is a stunning paradise hideaway where luxurious seclusion meets wild natural beauty. Maximum privacy is achieved with the concept of individual domains with each villa offering an abundance of indoor and outdoor living space. To complete your Maldivian experience, combine your resort stay with a cruise on the exclusive luxury catamaran, Four Seasons Explorer, which offers divers and non-divers alike a unique insight into the country's most remote marine and cultural attractions.

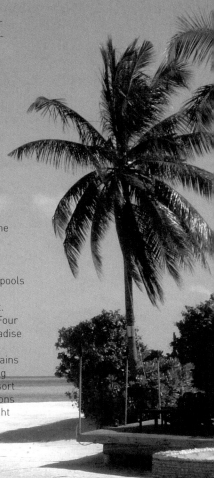

about the author

One of the world's leading surfing journalists, Tim Baker is a former editor of **Tracks** and **Surfing Life** magazines, and recipient of the Surfing Australia Hall of Fame Media Award. He is co-author of **Bustin' Down The Door**, the biography of the 1978 world surfing champion and ASP President, Wayne "Rabbit" Bartholomew. He is also editor of **Waves: Great Stories From The Surf**, an illustrated anthology of Australian surf writing. Tim has been shortlisted for the CUB Australian Sports Writing Awards and his work has appeared in **Rolling Stone**, **Playboy**, **GQ**, **Inside Sport**, **The Sydney Morning Herald**, **The Surfer's Journal**, and surfing magazines around the world. He is currently a senior contributor to **Surfing World**, **Surfing Life**, **Surfer's Path**, **US Surfer**, and **Surfing** magazines. With more than 20 years of working in the media and surfing magazines, he has also surfed and travelled throughout Indonesia, Hawaii, Central and South America, North America, Europe, Fiji, Tahiti, and Sri Lanka.